WEAPON

T0323091

THE G3 BATTLE RIFLE

LEROY THOMPSON

Series Editor Martin Pegler
Illustrated by Steve Noon & Alan Gilliland

OSPREY PUBLISHING
Bloomsbury Publishing Plc

Kemp House, Chawley Park, Oxford OX2 9PH, UK
29 Earlsfort Terrace, Dublin 2, Ireland
1385 Broadway, 5th Floor, New York, NY 10018, USA
Email: info@ospreypublishing.com
www.ospreypublishing.com

OSPREY is a trademark of Osprey Publishing Ltd

First published in Great Britain in 2019

© Osprey Publishing Ltd, 2019

A catalogue record for this book is available from the
British Library.

Print ISBN: 978 1 4728 2862 0
ePub: 978 1 4728 2863 7
ePDF: 978 1 4728 2864 4
XML: 978 1 4728 2865 1

Index by Rob Munro
Typeset by PDQ Digital Media Solutions, Bungay, UK
Printed and bound in India by Replika Press Private Ltd.

22 23 24 25 26   10 9 8 7 6 5 4 3 2

The Woodland Trust

Osprey Publishing supports the Woodland Trust, the UK's
leading woodland conservation charity.

www.ospreypublishing.com
To find out more about our authors and books visit our website.
Here you will find extracts, author interviews, details of
forthcoming events and the option to sign-up for our newsletter.

The Royal Armouries

The Royal Armouries is Britain's national museum of arms and
armour, and one of the most important museums of its type in
the world. Its origins lie in the Middle Ages, and at its core is the
celebrated collection originating in the nation's working arsenal,
assembled over many centuries at the Tower of London. In the
reign of Elizabeth I, selected items began to be arranged for
display to visitors, making the Royal Armouries heir to one of
the oldest deliberately created visitor attractions in the country.
The collection is now housed and displayed at three sites: the
White Tower at the Tower of London, a purpose-built museum in
Leeds, and Fort Nelson near Portsmouth. To find out more,
explore online at collections.royalarmouries.org

Artist's note

Readers may care to note that the original paintings from which
the colour plates in this book were prepared are available for
private sale. All reproduction copyright whatsoever is retained by
the publishers. All enquiries should be addressed to:

www.steve-noon.co.uk

The publishers regret that they can enter into no correspondence
upon this matter.

Dedication

In memory of my friend Ken Macswan, who came to the United
States from Scotland in his teens, then served in the 3rd Special
Forces Group (Airborne) and the 1st Aviation Brigade during the
Vietnam War. He spent the rest of his life as a professional
photographer and illustrator, and many of my books include
illustrations and photos by Ken. I will miss his good humour, wit
and talent.

Acknowledgements

The author would like to thank the following who assisted with
this book: Ken Choate; Michael Heidler; John Miller;
T.J. Mullin; Dena Sanders, Century International Arms; and
Blake Stevens, who deserves a special thanks for his outstanding
work on the roller-locking system.

Front cover, above: A right-side view of an early-production G3
from May 1960, though the serial number puts it as being
produced in April 1960. The rifle presents an interesting
combination of features, including a laminated-wood buttstock,
black polymer pistol grip, diopter rear sight, folding bipod and
the early-style flash hider. However, it lacks the reinforcing rib
around the magazine well that began with June 1960 production.
The handguard actually appears to be of the type which,
combined with the folding bipod, was used on CETME
Model 58 rifles. This combination of handguard and bipod was
also used on some HK prototype rifles. In fact, this appears to be
the sheet-metal handguard in the 1959 G3 specifications.
However, the bipod was deleted in these specifications. It is
possible that earlier parts were still being used up, thus
accounting for the interesting combination of features. (USNPS
Photo, Springfield Armory National Historic Site, SPAR 3649)

Front cover, below: An Iranian Revolutionary Guard on duty in
the Niavaran Palace Complex (former home of the exiled Shah)
in December 1979. His rifle appears to be a G3A6, the standard
version produced by Defense Industries Organization. What
appears to be a rack number in Farsi is on the stock, which may
indicate that this is a former Iranian Army rifle. (Alex Bowie/
Getty Images)

Title-page image: These Cold War-era Bundeswehr troops on an
exercise in West Germany are armed with the G3SG/1
Scharfschützengewehr ('sharpshooting rifle'), an accurized
version of the G3 mounting the Zeiss Diavari-DA 1.5–6×36
telescopic sight with STANAG (NATO Standardization
Agreement) claw-mount assembly. The G3SG/1 has a special set
trigger and a longer stock with a dual-stage buffer and adjustable
cheek rest (Johnston & Nelson 2010: 445). The Bundeswehr
later adopted the MSG3 (MSG standing for *Militärisches
Scharfschützen Gewehr* – 'military sharpshooting rifle') as a more
specialized sniping rifle. The MSG3 has a 600mm-long barrel
and features an improved scope mount, cheek riser and
adjustable stock length. The most accurate version of the G3
intended for sniping is the PSG1 (*Präzisionsschützengewehr* –
'precision shooter rifle'), a semi-automatic weapon with a light
trigger pull, fully adjustable stock and 6×42mm telescopic sight.
(Calle Hesslefors/ullstein bild via Getty Images)

CONTENTS

INTRODUCTION

During the Cold War, the Gewehr 3 (G3) battle rifle served alongside the FN FAL and the M14 as one of the world's pre-eminent combat rifles, notably among NATO countries. While versions of the FN FAL were adopted by Belgium, Luxembourg, the Netherlands, Portugal, Turkey, the United Kingdom and, for a short period, West Germany, the G3 was adopted by Denmark, Greece, Norway, Portugal (to replace the FAL), Spain, Turkey and West Germany. After the 5.56×45mm round became the NATO standard in 1980, versions of the G3 designed for that round were adopted by some countries, such as Greece and Portugal, that had previously used the G3. Although the G3 was replaced in German military service by the 5.56×45mm G36 assault rifle from 1997, the G3 variants remain in use today with the armed forces of Germany and others as a DMR (designated marksman rifle).

Developed in Spain at CETME (Centro de Estudios Técnicos de Materiales Especiales: Centre for Technical Studies of Special Materials) by a team that included some German engineers who had moved to Spain after 1945, the Modelo 1958 was the Spanish forerunner of the G3. It used a roller-delayed blowback action, similar to that used on the German 7.92×57mm MG 42 machine gun, which offered an alternative to the gas-actuated piston system used in many other military rifles. More significantly, the roller action had been used in the German 7.92×33mm StG 45(M)

A left-side view of the G3 depicted on the front cover. The G3's plastic pistol grip, evident here, is one of the more comfortable battle-rifle pistol grips. (USNPS Photo, Springfield Armory National Historic Site, SPAR 3649)

An interesting view of German *Panzergrenadiere* (mechanized infantry) in September 2010; the soldier at left has a G36 assault rifle while the others have the G3A3 battle rifle with slim tropical handguard. In simple terms, an assault rifle is chambered for an intermediate cartridge that allows the weapon to be more compact, use a larger-capacity magazine and be more controllable during fully automatic fire; the smaller size of the cartridge permits a soldier to carry more rounds of ammunition as his basic combat load. A battle rifle, on the other hand, is chambered for a full-power rifle round, but is bulker and heavier; it normally has a smaller-capacity magazine, is harder to control during fully automatic fire, and the size and weight of the ammunition restricts the soldier to carrying fewer rounds in his basic combat load. On the positive side, the battle rifle gives greater range and has greater striking power. The classic examples of the assault rifle during the Cold War were the AK-47 and M16, while the pre-eminent battle rifles were the G3, FN FAL and M14. (Bundeswehr-Fotos/Wikimedia/CC BY 2.0)

assault rifle, though only prototypes of that weapon had been produced before the end of World War II. Production of the CETME began in Spain in 1957 and the weapon was adopted by the Spanish armed forces. Initially, the West Germans had planned to adopt the CETME, but in 1956 adopted the FN FAL instead. However, in January 1959, the CETME was adopted by the Bundeswehr as the G3. Although the initial production run of CETME rifles in Spain had been chambered for a lower-powered cartridge, the Heckler & Koch (HK)-produced rifle adopted in West Germany as the G3 took the 7.62×51mm NATO cartridge.

HK produced rifles for the Bundeswehr, as well as for export to at least 50 other countries. Countries that produced the G3 under licence from HK included Greece, Mexico, Norway, Pakistan, Portugal, Saudi Arabia, Sweden and Turkey. Having imported G3 rifles before the Iranian Revolution toppled the Shah in February 1979, Iran has continued to produce the weapon. Estimates of total production of the G3 (and CETME) around the world run to at least seven million, but likely many more. It has also proven a very popular semi-automatic rifle in the United States and other countries where civilians can own sporting versions of military rifles.

HK produced the HK33, a 5.56×45mm assault rifle based on the G3, from 1968. This is a left-side view of the 5.56×45mm HK53, a derivative of the HK33 that was especially popular with British special forces. (Author)

DEVELOPMENT
Towards the G3

ORIGINS

From Gerät 06H to StG 45(M)

The genesis of the G3 rifle can be traced to German experimental *Sturmgewehr* designs of World War II developed by weapons manufacturers including Haenel, Steyr, Grossfuss, Spreewerk, Gustloff and Mauser; these rifles were chambered for an intermediate-powered cartridge, the 7.92×33mm *Kurz* round (Johnston & Nelson 2010: 369). Although the Haenel design was chosen for production as the StG 44 assault rifle, it was considered expensive to produce and thus development work continued on the Mauser Gerät 06H. Also chambered for the 7.92×33mm *Kurz* round, the Gerät 06H was intended as a replacement for the StG 44 that would be cheaper and quicker to manufacture.

Initially, the Gerät 06H design incorporated the roller-locked short recoil system used in the MG 42 machine gun, but with a fixed barrel and a conventional gas-actuated piston rod. To simplify the design even more, the gas system was eliminated, resulting in the 'H' of the designation to indicate *halbverriegelt* ('half-locked'). This system allowed the bolt to begin its rearward travel while the bullet was still travelling down the barrel and the case was under full pressure from the gases; as a result, there were problems with case heads separating. The solution was to cut flutes in the chamber to allow the gases to 'float' the front and neck of the case to ease extraction. This system has continued in use in many HK firearms and results in the distinctive striations found on spent cases ejected from such weapons.

The roller-locking system was not invented by Mauser, but dated to the Siemens-Schuckert roller-lock patent of 1929 (Stevens 2006: 2). In 1942, Mauser began work on a fully locked roller system. Although

The Mauser Gerät 06H. (Courtesy US National Park Service, Springfield Armory National Historic Site, SPAR 1592)

Mauser experimented with this system, engineers were also aware of the half-locked system used in the MG 42 machine gun and based on a Polish 1937 patent (Stevens 2006: 4).

In the early prototypes of the Gerät 06H that still used a gas piston, a pair of rollers in the bolt head were designed to lock by camming into a pair of locking recesses. When the rifle was fired, the gas piston caused the rollers to disengage, allowing the bolt to travel to the rear extracting the spent case and feeding a new round into the chamber (Johnston & Nelson 2010: 370). The Heereswaffenamt (German Army Weapons Office) wanted a simpler design that eliminated the gas piston, however. The roller-delayed blowback system chosen to eliminate the piston did not require the bolt ever to be fully locked closed. Instead, the rollers slowed the rearward movement of the bolt as they disengaged from the locking recess. Rearward bolt movement was further inhibited by the angle at which the rollers pressed against the bolt body. Straight blowback operations with a rifle-calibre cartridge would put too much strain on the action, but by retarding the impulse of the bolt with the rollers, some of its momentum was dissipated.

Three prototype Gerät 06 rifles were tested, with one successfully firing 7,000 rounds on full-auto. As a result, Mauser received an order for 30 rifles to undergo field trials, but the war ended before they could be delivered (Johnston & Nelson 2010: 371). This design, once it had been approved by the Heereswaffenamt, was designated the StG 45(M), the 'M' standing for Mauser (Stevens 2006: 35). The design of the StG 45(M) relied heavily on stampings and used welded joints that were not subject to direct stress during firing, thus simplifying production even more. Production of the StG 45(M) required approximately half the time and materials needed to manufacture the StG 44 (Johnston & Nelson 2010: 371). According to Mauser employee Ott von Lossnitzer, who was debriefed by Allied intelligence after World War II, savings in production time were even greater when compared to the 7.92×57mm Kar 98k bolt-action rifle: 3–4 hours for the new weapon, compared to 12–14 hours (Stevens 2006: 57). Conversely, Ernst Altenburger, the StG 45(M)'s chief designer, stated that the team at Mauser estimated that it would take 6.25 hours to produce an StG 45(M) rifle (Johnston & Nelson 2010: 388).

The G3's fluted chamber leaves distinctive striations on fired brass cases. (Author)

The StG 45(M) falls into Allied hands

During April 1945, machinery and prototypes for various Mauser designs, as well as 200 engineers and skilled craftsman from the Mauser factory in

Oberndorf, were loaded on a special 29-car train, which left Oberndorf during the night of 19/20 April for Ötzal in the Austrian Alps, arriving on 30 April. There the train was discovered on 1 June by a joint American and British team from the Combined Intelligence Objectives Subcommittee (Stevens 2006: 59). After the end of hostilities, Mauser engineers were interrogated about various projects, including the StG 45(M). According to a report prepared by Allied intelligence officers, there were four complete StG 45(M) rifles and sets of parts for an additional 30 on the train. Reportedly, German engineers and craftsmen assembled at least some of the parts into complete rifles, which went into collections in the United States, the United Kingdom and France; blueprints were also distributed among the Allies (Stevens 2006: 61). Some of these rifles appear to have entered the collections held by the Springfield Armory National Historic Site in the United States.

The Mauser factory at Oberndorf was captured by the French Army on 20 April 1945. As soon as was practicable, the French began producing weapons on the Mauser machinery using Mauser employees who had remained in the area. As part of the re-armament of the French armed forces, HSc, P 08 and P 38 pistols and Kar 98k rifles, as well as some .22 training rifles, were produced at the factory for more than a year (Stevens 2006: 99). Production ceased when the machinery and tooling from Mauser was disassembled and divided among the Allied countries, including the Soviet Union. Beginning in May 1945, a joint British, American and French ordnance intelligence team gathered intelligence on Mauser research and development work and prototype weapons (Johnston & Nelson 2010: 393).

The United States and France were both interested in the StG 45(M) project and gathered as much information as possible about the design. It was France, however, that hired Mauser engineers Theodor Löffler and Ludwig Vorgrimler to pursue the design at the Centre d'Études d'Armement de Mulhouse (CEAM), later redesignated Atelier Mécanique de Mulhouse (AME). By the end of March 1948, a total of 138 Mauser engineers and skilled craftsmen had moved to Mulhouse (Stevens 2006: 107).

The 7.92×33mm StG 45(M) assault rifle disassembled into its primary component parts, as shown in a Springfield Armory reference photograph. (Courtesy US National Park Service, Springfield Armory National Historic Site, 019-058-2001/ORD-59)

Löffler and Vorgrimler were assigned to the 'CEAM Light Weapons Group' with the mission of designing two new weapons: Project 701, a heavy machine pistol, and Project 702, a self-loading carbine (Stevens 2006: 108). Among the resulting designs were the AMI Model I of 1948, AMI Model 1949, AMI Model II and AMI Model 1950. These designs were chambered for either the US .30 Carbine cartridge or the French 7.65×35mm experimental round. The AMI Model 1949 and AMI Model II both fired from an open bolt (Johnston & Nelson 2010: 394).

Designed by Vorgrimler, the AMI Model I used a roller-locking system but incorporated a folding buttstock similar in appearance to that of the German 9×19mm MP 40 submachine gun. Although the AMI Model I was chambered for the French 7.65×35mm round initially, in 1950 it was also tested in .30 Carbine calibre. The AMI Model 1949 was only chambered in .30 Carbine calibre. An interesting feature of the Model 1949 was that it fired from a closed bolt on semi-auto and an open bolt on full-auto (Johnston & Nelson 2010: 278–79).

The AMI Model II and Model 1950 were both chambered for the US .30 Carbine round. As with the other AMI designs, these two used the roller-locking systems. Prototypes of the Model 1950 most closely resembled the StG 45(M). All of the models prior to the Model 1950 had been evaluated at Établissement d'expériences techniques de Versailles (ETVS) during March 1949, but none was approved for further development (Stevens 2006: 121).

A new design by Löffler that incorporated features from the various earlier designs was initially designated the Model II/3, but would evolve into the Model 1950 chambered for the US .30 Carbine cartridge. The Model 1950 retained the roller-delayed blowback action and employed a closed bolt for both semi- and full-auto fire. During its development, variant prototypes of the Model 1950 were produced, notably one with the cocking handle on the right side and another with it on the left side. One notable feature of the Model 1950 was a side-folding buttstock. (Stevens 2006: 131–32).

The various roller-delayed blowback designs did not result in a weapon that would be adopted by the French, however. Instead, the French adopted the MAT 49 submachine gun, a 9×19mm blowback design, and the MAS 49 semi-automatic rifle, a direct-impingement gas-operated design in 7.5×54mm French calibre.

The Spanish intervene

The roller-delayed blowback design gained a new lease of life in Spain. In 1949, while work on designs using the roller-delayed blowback system was still in progress, the Spanish approached Werner Heynen, the former head of automatic-weapons development within Dr Albert Speer's Reich Ministry of Armaments and War Production. Heynen was charged with assembling a group of German scientists to develop an automatic rifle to replace the M98/43 Mauser bolt-action rifles then in use by the Spanish armed forces. Heynen was put in charge of a development programme for CETME in Madrid. Ludwig Vorgrimler left France and eventually joined the group at CETME in September 1950 (Stevens 2006: 139).

Original Spanish requirements for the cartridge to be chambered in the new rifle specified that it must be accurate at 1,000m yet be viable in a rifle weighing under 3kg. Another German, Günther Voss, formerly a ballistics expert for the Luftwaffe, developed the 7.92×41mm CETME cartridge to meet the Spanish requirements. This cartridge used a long bullet weighing only 100 grains (6.48g) at 819.91m/sec. The 7.92×41mm round generated less recoil, thus allowing the rifle to be controlled better on full-auto fire; despite its low bullet weight it remained accurate to 1,000m (Stevens 2006: 140). However, Spain was a NATO member and the standard NATO cartridge was the 7.62×51mm NATO round.

Two CETME designs were developed simultaneously to meet the Spanish requirements for a new rifle. The first was the Modelo 1, a locked breech, roller-locked rifle designed by the German engineer Hartmut Menneking, while the second, the Modelo 2, was a half-locked, retarded-blowback design based on the StG 45(M) and designed by Vorgrimler (Johnston & Nelson 2010: 394). Both designs resembled the StG 45(M), with the Modelo 2 being closer in appearance to the later CETME design that would evolve into the G3. The Modelo 1 used a 'brace-wing' flap-locking system similar to that of the World War II Gew 43 semi-automatic rifle (Stevens 2006: 140). The design of the Modelo 1 began early in 1950, but Vorgrimler could not start work on the Modelo 2 until he arrived in Spain in September that year (Stevens 2006: 141). One problem Vorgrimler encountered was the lack of Spanish factories capable of carrying out the operations necessary to produce the stamped steel required for the design of the Modelo 2. He improvised by using the test workshop of a factory near Madrid to produce the stampings for the prototypes of the Modelo 2 (Stevens 2006: 141).

Three prototypes of each model were produced, though it took two years to do so. The prototypes of the Modelo 1 were produced at Fábrica National de Toledo and those of the Modelo 2 at Armamento de Aviación de Pinto (Stevens 2006: 142). Werner Heynen, former director of Gustloffwerke and later CETME's head of design, attributed this long development time to a combination of factors: the lack of a machine shop with experience in producing prototypes for research and development; the fact that military weapons factories lay hundreds of kilometres apart;

The CETME Model A in 7.62×51mm calibre is shown in this photograph dated 9 June 1954. One noteworthy feature of the Model A was that it fired from an open bolt on full-auto, but a closed bolt on semi-auto. The bipod folded back to form the forearm. The 20- and 30-round magazines are shown along with the grenade launcher and the grenade-launcher sight. (Courtesy US National Park Service, Springfield Armory National Historic Site, A99444)

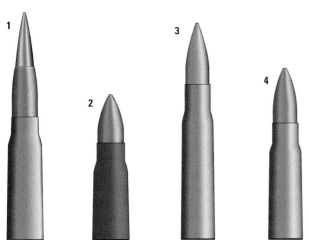

The 7.92×41mm CETME round (**1**) was a bridge between the German 7.92×33mm *Kurz* round (**2**) developed for the *Sturmgewehr* assault rifles and the later 7.62×51mm NATO round (**3**) that would be chambered in the G3. The Soviet 7.62×39mm round (**4**) and the 5.56×45mm NATO round (**5**) are also shown for comparison.

and the shortage of skilled engineers and craftsmen (Stevens 2006: 141). It should be noted, however, that Vorgrimler worked with a number of skilled Spanish engineers, notably Luis Wilhelmi and Ignacio del Riego. The initial prototype of the Modelo 1 was presented to the Alto Estado Mayor (AEM: Defence High Command) on 14 September 1950, while that of the Modelo 2 was presented on 15 December (Stevens 2006: 142).

Though delivered second, the prototype of the Modelo 2 was demonstrated first to Generalissimo Francisco Franco on 2 July 1951 (Johnston & Nelson 2010: 396). Firing out to 600m, the Modelo 2 impressed Franco and observing officers. Just two days later, on 4 July, 30 more Modelo 2 rifles, designated the *Null-Serie* (zero series) by the AEM, were ordered for broader testing, as were 150,000 rounds of ammunition (Stevens 2006: 143). During production of this additional batch of 30 rifles, it was discovered that Armamento de Aviación de Pinto had used different materials for the rollers that delayed the opening of the breech than were called for in the technical drawings and specifications, and that the hardening process had not been carried out in the required manner (Stevens 2006: 143). The firm was ordered to adhere rigorously to technical specifications in the future in order to avoid excessive wear to the rollers. During production of the additional rifles, research was conducted into the use of optical sights, bayonet mounting systems, devices for firing rifle grenades and a polymer stock (Stevens 2006: 144).

The prototype of the Modelo 1 began trials on 13 March 1952, with a demonstration to Franco, followed during the next few days by demonstrations to high-ranking West German officers and American representatives. According to Vorgrimler, however, the Modelo 1 was dogged by problems, and was not demonstrated, only shown; consequently, it was determined that three further Modelo 2 prototypes should be assembled and undergo sustained-fire testing (Stevens 2006: 144).

During work on the 30 *Null-Serie* Modelo 2 rifles, an old problem arose that had been encountered with the Mauser Gerät 06H: bolt bounce, which caused premature breakage of locking parts. Vorgrimler developed

THE US VERDICT

In July 1954, two *Null-Serie* CETME Model A rifles and their 7.92×41mm (aka 7.92×40mm) ammunition were tested at Aberdeen Proving Ground in Maryland for general functioning and handling, accuracy and endurance, including withstanding cold, rain and dust (Stevens 2006: 152). The US evaluators were especially interested in the cost savings offered by the use of stampings, and also in the roller-delayed blowback operating system.

In fact, the concise description of the CETME's operation provided in the report by ordnance engineer L.F. Moore is worth quoting, as the system remained virtually the same in the rifle's later incarnation as the G3:

> The rifle operates on a delayed-blow-back principle. The bolt is assembled to the bolt carrier and it is permitted to move longitudinally 0.25 inch [6.35mm] independently of the bolt carrier. The bolt contains two rollers which, when the bolt is in its forward position, are forced outward into recesses in the locking ring by a cam attached to the bolt carrier. When a round is fired, the bolt is forced rearward. A cam surface on the locking ring forces the rollers inward against the cam which in turn is forced to the rear with the bolt carrier. The bolt carrier assembly weighs 1.52 pounds [0.69kg] as compared with 0.25 pounds [0.11kg] for the bolt assembly. A large operating spring is employed. The spring is made of wire having a diameter of approximately 0.055 inch [1.40mm]; it is about 23 inches [584mm] in length, and it has an outside diameter of 0.45 inch [11.43mm]. The spring is positioned within a tube, which is partially closed at the forward end and is assembled to the top of the bolt carrier. The tube protrudes forward from the bolt carrier a distance of 10.8 inches [274.32mm]. A 0.315-inch [8.00mm] diameter tube attached to the stock group serves as a guide for the spring. Indentations in each side of the receiver form guide rods on which the bolt group reciprocates. (Moore 1954)

I have found this to be the most concise and clear explanation of the roller-delayed blowback operating system in my research.

Overall, the Aberdeen Proving Ground assessment of the CETME was lukewarm. Among the criticisms were: there were a large number of pins and springs that could easily be lost; ergonomics were not good; the rifle lacked a forearm; there were a number of failures to feed during test-firing; the sights were 'objectionable'; the magazines were difficult to load; and the rifle was susceptible to excessive fouling after firing a large number of rounds. Nevertheless, Vorgrimler, who had observed the trials, pronounced them a great success (Stevens 2006: 158). On the positive side, the low recoil of the *Null-Serie* rifles chambered for the 7.92×41mm cartridge was noted by those testing the CETME at Aberdeen Proving Ground.

a 'recoil block' comprising a spring-loaded locking lever attached laterally to the breechblock carrier. This locking lever hooked together the breech mechanism rollers with the guide piece and breech head. This kept the hammer from hitting the breechblock carrier during recoil, thus causing a misfire. As a result of this improvement, the Spanish authorities increased the order for *Null-Serie* rifles to 100, then again to 120 (Stevens 2006: 144). At the time, however, CETME did not have the capacity to produce even this limited number of rifles.

Plans for production of the *Null-Serie* weapons were influenced by the wish to avoid as much as possible the need for special machinery and highly skilled workers. Additionally, there was a desire to use to the greatest extent possible materials available in Spain. Spanish politics and connections also played a part in the plans to produce the rifle. Eventually, production of parts for the *Null-Serie* was parcelled out to various subcontractors. CETME produced the sheet-metal receiver housing and assembly at its own test shop, however, to allow the project engineers to monitor production for any problems in this, the most difficult and important part of the rifle to be manufactured. Those tools used to produce the sheet-metal parts for the *Null-Serie* weapons, as well as critical gauges, jigs and fixtures, were designed to be used when full-scale production began. Additionally, a facility was developed to test all

Views of the 7.92×41mm *Null-Serie* CETME Model A rifles tested by the Americans at Aberdeen Proving Ground in July 1954. (Courtesy US National Park Service, Springfield Armory National Historic Site, A99059)

subcontracted parts to ensure that they conformed to specifications to allow interchangeability (Stevens 2006: 146).

In July 1952, the decision was made to discontinue work on the Modelo 1 design and proceed with the Modelo 2, which would eventually be designated as the CETME Model A (Johnston & Nelson 2010: 396). In November that year, *Null-Serie* rifles first underwent testing, with 11,000 rounds being fired during sustained fire. The tests were deemed successful, though the rate of barrel erosion was deemed too high (Stevens 2006: 146). The CETME, as the rifle would be designated, continued to undergo testing over the next year, with the design being adjusted based on performance. By 1 April 1954, the CETME was deemed proven enough that some troops marched with it in a parade celebrating the 15th anniversary of Franco's victory in the Spanish Civil War (Johnston & Nelson 2010: 400). It is important to note that at this point, the CETME was still chambered for the 7.92×41mm round.

International interest grows

Despite the negative assessment offered by the Americans, the Spanish were satisfied with the *Null-Serie* rifles they had been testing and were ready to commence mass production of the rifle. As a result, stamping tools were ordered from Württembergische Metallwarenfabrik (WMF) in Geislingen, West Germany (Stevens 2006: 159).

There was interest in the CETME design from other countries as well. Prior to the establishment of the Bundeswehr in November 1955, the Bundesgrenzschutz (BGS; Federal Border Guard), founded on 14 March 1951, was West Germany's primary armed force. After witnessing a demonstration of the CETME in December 1953, BGS personnel tested two of the *Null-Serie* rifles in mid-1954 (Stevens 2006: 164). These tests were followed, in January 1955, by the demonstration of one of the early CETME Type A rifles, which were still prototypes firing from a closed bolt on semi-auto and an open bolt on full-auto. The BGS expressed an interest in the CETME design, but specified that that they wanted a rifle chambered in 7.62×41mm (Johnston & Nelson 2010: 400). There seems to have been some miscommunication here, as what the West Germans wanted was a rifle chambered for the US T65 NATO cartridge, generally known as the 7.62×51mm NATO round. Johnston and Nelson speculate that the miscommunication may have occurred because the BGS was evaluating the rifle initially based on their own criteria, rather than those of the Bundeswehr, which had not yet been founded (Johnston & Nelson 2010: 401).

The need for a NATO standard chambering was made clear when West German representatives went to Madrid to order 40 CETME rifles for troop trials for the Bundeswehr, which would be activated on 12 November 1955. Anxious to receive a lucrative contract from the West Germans, CETME pushed Vorgrimler to alter the CETME rifle to take the T65 cartridge, even though this would have involved a complete redesign of the bolt and a lengthening of the receiver due to more powerful recoil. Instead, in an effort to rush a test example for the West Germans, a *Null-Serie* rifle was converted to fire the NATO round. The thin carbon steel of the receiver quickly developed cracks, however, and the rollers were crushed. It was estimated that the rifle would only last for a few hundred rounds if used with the more powerful cartridge (Stevens 2006: 166).

CETME's solution was to change the angle at which the rollers moved and to load a lighter bullet with a lighter powder charge in a 7.62×51mm NATO case (Johnston & Nelson 2010: 403). Designated the 'CETME-NATO' cartridge (CSP-003), this round had a bullet that weighed 112.6 grains (7.30g), as compared to 143.5 grains (9.30g) for an SS-77 NATO round (Stevens 2006: 167). Velocity for the two cartridges out to 1,000m remained very close: at 1,000m the remaining velocity of the CSP-003 bullet was 272m/sec and that of the SS-77 NATO bullet was 271m/sec (Stevens 2006: 168). The rifle chambered for the CSP-003 was designated the CETME Model A. It should be noted that the lighter CSP-003 round actually conformed to the assault-rifle concept of a cartridge that was lighter than that of a traditional battle rifle, but more powerful than a submachine-gun or carbine cartridge. The lighter assault-rifle cartridge would allow better control of the weapon during full-auto fire.

Heckler & Koch enters the scene

West German interest in the CETME design prompted the Spaniards to seek a West German firm to manufacture the rifle. Logically, since the CETME had evolved from a Mauser design and had been incubated by Mauser engineers, the reconstituted Mauser firm was approached with a view to producing the CETME in West Germany, but Mauser was not interested. As a result, the CETME delegation looked to another arms manufacturer, though a fledgling one, that was also located in Oberndorf: Heckler & Koch (Stevens 2006: 164).

A view of the G3 bolt group with a close-up of the rollers that are critical to the weapon's delayed-blowback action. The G3's roller-delayed blowback locking system is viewed positively by some users, but negatively by others. It is argued that this locking system offers some mitigation of recoil, especially when the weapon is fired on full-auto. Advocates also argue that the roller-delayed blowback system offers a very high degree of reliability and is also easier to maintain than gas-operated rifles such as the FAL. (Author)

Heckler & Koch (HK) had been formed in 1948 by two former Mauser employees – Edmund Heckler and Theodor Koch. Initially, due to the post-World War II restriction on arms production, the company produced sewing machines and machine tools. Skilled workers were drawn from former Mauser employees, and HK entered the arms industry in 1953–54 by producing gauges for the Swiss (Stevens 2006: 162).

At a demonstration of the CETME rifle during 17–23 January 1955, Generals Schneider, Henrici and Kittel represented West Germany and the Vice Chief of AEM and the Spanish Ambassador to West Germany represented Spain. Also present were HK representatives, as the firm would be the likely producer of the rifle if it was adopted by West Germany. As the Bundeswehr had not yet officially come into existence, this demonstration was conducted under the auspices of the BGS. In addition to the CETME, the FN FAL was also demonstrated (Stevens 2006: 165).

Reports after the demonstration were very favourable to the CETME, though the CSP-003 cartridge did not make such a good impression. For the rifle to be considered for adoption by West Germany certain changes were deemed necessary, including a stronger bipod, a magazine with a capacity of no more than 25 rounds (the test CETME magazines held 32 rounds) and different sights, with the rear sight closer to the shooter and with a 'U' rather than a 'V' notch. No muzzle brake was desired for use with the T65 NATO round. The West Germans wanted a 7.62mm round that matched the NATO T65 in its external dimensions, yet would have recoil similar to that of the German 7.92×33mm *Kurz* cartridge used in the StG 44. A shorter, ballistically improved bullet was specified, with an effective range of 600m (Stevens 2006: 166).

West German interest in the CETME continued with a second demonstration of the CETME Model A in June 1955. The rifle was demonstrated with versions firing the CSP-003 cartridge as well as the T65 NATO standard round. (It is not clear whether separate rifles were demonstrated, or if it was shown that by switching out some components, the Model A could function reliably and safely with the T65 round.) The rifle satisfied the West German evaluators, who placed an order for 250 rifles for troop trials. Over the next few months, demonstrations of the Model A were also given for the Swedes, French and Italians; while the Swedes would adopt the G3 and produce it under licence, the French and Italians did not (Stevens 2006: 169).

Joint Spanish–German production begins

Based on the favourable impression made by the CETME Model A, an agreement was concluded for joint Spanish–German production of the CETME rifle in April 1954. The initial BGS order for 5,000 rifles was placed on 19 July 1955 (Stevens 2006: 174). As Spain lacked the industrial capacity to produce the rifle alone, it was intended that HK and WMF would undertake production of those components of the rifle produced in West Germany, while at least a dozen Spanish companies would produce parts under the umbrella of CETME (Stevens 2006: 176).

As the date on which the West German Bundeswehr would be activated approached, the BGS turned over responsibility for CETME acquisition to the Bundesministerium der Verteidigung (BMV: Federal Defence Ministry), which demanded that the rifle be designed for the full-power 7.62×51mm NATO cartridge. As a result, the design of the CETME Model A had to be adapted with a recoil buffer and strengthening of various parts of the design (Stevens 2006: 178). Delays – resulting from organizing the various subcontractors, acquiring tooling and blueprints, and strengthening the rifle to take the 7.62×51mm NATO round – eventually exhausted the patience of the West Germans. On 17 January 1956, the BGS cancelled the 5,000-rifle order (Stevens 2006: 183).

Delays in development of the CETME combined with the pressure to adopt a rifle for the Bundeswehr resulted in the adoption of the FN FAL to meet West Germany's immediate needs. The BGS had already evaluated the version of the FAL with wooden furniture and a pronged flash hider that had been developed for Canada in December 1954, and again with rifles provided by FN in January 1955. In both sets of trials, the FAL performed well, resulting in the BGS ordering 100 of the Canadian-type FALs, but without flash hiders, for further evaluation (Stevens 2006: 181–82). On 13 November 1956, the Bundeswehr placed an order for 100,000 FN FAL rifles from the FN factory in Liège, Belgium. These rifles were produced between April 1957 and May 1958, and were designated as the Gewehr 1 (G1) (Johnston & Nelson 2010: 403).

Gerhard Schröder, West Germany's Minister of the Interior, inspects an example of the Gewehr 1 (G1) rifle issued to the BGS in July 1956. Once the Bundeswehr was established a large order for 100,000 FALs was placed on 13 November 1956. (Keystone/Hulton Archive/Getty Images)

West German troop trials

The BMV remained interested in the CETME rifle design, however, and ordered 400 examples in April 1956, for exhaustive troop trials. The parts for these rifles would be produced jointly between CETME and HK. In addition to the 400 trial CETME rifles, 1,600 magazines and spare parts were ordered (Johnston & Nelson 2010: 404). As the 400-rifle order was viewed as the preliminary for large future consignments, a plan was developed carefully setting out the 56 procedures that would be necessary to produce the rifle. During production in West Germany, a quality-control commission carefully monitored any difficulties, which included wandering point of impact during testing for accuracy and cracks in stamped receiver housings. The constant monitoring of production delayed the delivery of the 400 test rifles, however. Contributing to the production problems was the fact that Ludwig Vorgrimler, who had been lead development engineer on the CETME rifle, had left CETME for Mauser (Stevens 2006: 191).

The 400 trial CETME rifles were delivered by December 1956, after which competitive trials against the FN FAL (G1) were carried out. In January 1957, the German magazine *Der Spiegel* reported that the joint CETME/HK rifle had performed well (Stevens 2006: 198). After extensive testing, however, the Bundesamt für Wehrtechnik und Beschaffung (BWB: Federal Office of Defence Technology and Procurement) ordered significant changes before the CETME rifle could be considered for adoption. The most noteworthy of these changes were lightening the rifle and changing it to fire only from a closed bolt, rather than from an open bolt on full-auto. The rifle that incorporated these changes was designated the CETME Model B (Johnston & Nelson 2010: 404).

As a result of the troop trials, the BWB developed a list of 17 additions and improvements that would be required before more extensive troop trials could take place. These consisted of: a combination flash hider/ grenade launcher; a stronger front-sight protector; a rear sight of either flip-up or diopter type; a latch for the carrying handle; a change in the positions of the selector lever detents; a spent-case deflector; changing the metal buttplate to rubber; simplifying the pistol grip for ease of production; changing the sling attachment points; lengthening the cocking lever;

A CETME rifle produced in August 1956 with the bipod deployed and 25-round magazine in place. (Collector Grade Publications)

OTHER BUNDESWEHR CONTENDERS

Although the best-known rifles tested to arm the Bundeswehr were the CETME (G3) and the FN FAL (G1), there were two others in the running. The SIG SG 510 (G2) battle rifle was ordered in a quantity of 50: 40 with rubber buttstocks and ten with wooden buttstocks. Chambered for 7.62×51mm NATO ammunition, the G2 was a version of the service rifle adopted by the Swiss, the 7.5×55mm Stgw 57 battle rifle. The 7.62×51mm version as marketed to various countries was usually designated as the SG 510-4. The 50 SIG rifles were delivered to the BWB on 19 December 1957; but although the G2 was given substantial testing, at 4.37kg unloaded weight it was deemed too heavy for West German adoption (Stevens 2006: 215).

Also tested was an American rifle, the ArmaLite AR-10 (G4), also in 7.62×51mm NATO calibre. Five examples of the G4, which had been produced in the Netherlands under licence from the ArmaLite Division of the Fairchild Aircraft Corporation, were acquired for testing late in 1957. Tested in adverse conditions and given a 10,000-round full-auto test-firing, they performed reasonably well. In fact, 400 additional G4 rifles were ordered for further testing, indicating that the design was considered promising, and, unlike the G2, the G4 was light – in the region of 3.3kg, depending on variant. This order was soon cancelled, however. Eventually, 135 G4 rifles were delivered to various West German training schools in August and September 1958 for more extensive testing. The fact that sniper and light-machine-gun versions of the AR-10 were available was a selling point for the West Germans; but though the West Germans expressed interest, the Dutch manufacturer, Artillerie-Inrichtingen, was not geared up for large-scale production and could not readily incorporate changes. As a result, the AR-10 did not remain in competition for large West German military contracts (Stevens 2006: 216).

In 1957, 50 SIG SG 510 battle rifles, designated the G2, were ordered for testing by the Bundeswehr. Like the G3, the G2 had a version of the roller-delayed action. Because of the G2's weight, however, it did not receive serious consideration. Shown here is the PE 57, the semi-automatic civilian version of the SG 510 rifle. A military version of the rifle was also offered for military export in 7.62×51mm or for civilian sale as the SIG AMT (Stevens 2006: 455–59). (Author)

changing the outer shape of the barrel, the recoil spring guide, the pistol-grip attachment pin, the buffer system, the shape of the buttstock and the trigger system's safety lever; and a more ergonomic cocking lever (Johnston & Nelson 2010: 408).

Based on the optimistic view that the rifle would perform well, further improvements were specified after completion of the troop trials, including: a stronger bipod; special hand protection; a more ergonomic pistol grip; and reduced weight (Johnston & Nelson 2010: 408). A third phase of improvements was specified once production had begun and there had been even more extensive testing, namely: altering the trigger mechanism so the rifle could be cocked with the safety applied; providing a lighter, 20-round magazine; and adding a bolt hold-open when the magazine was empty (Johnston & Nelson 2010: 408).

HK made changes to the CETME specifications as the company began production of the Model B. Most noteworthy was the change from low-carbon steel to high-grade alloy steel in order to withstand the greater stress of the 7.62×51mm NATO cartridge. Also strengthened were the bolt head, bolt carrier, locking piece and locking rollers. Additionally, to allow the rifle to function reliably, 20 roller sizes were produced to be selected as needed for each rifle (Johnston & Nelson 2010: 408).

Spain adopts the CETME

While CETME and HK had been working to sell the CETME rifle to the Germans, the Spanish armed forces had been testing the rifle for their own adoption. As a result, the Spanish Army adopted the CETME Model B as the *Fusil de Asalto CETME Modelo 1958 de 7'62mm* on 27 September 1957. Adoption by the Spanish Navy followed on 16 January 1958 and by the Spanish Air Force on 26 July that year. As originally adopted, the Spanish rifle chambered the reduced-power 7.62×51mm CETME cartridge rather than the more powerful 7.62×51mm NATO cartridge. Improvements to the rifle included a different carrying handle, a strengthened bipod and a metal handguard. A special version with a folding stock was designed for airborne and other special troops. A telescopic sight was also available and a firing-port version designated the Model R for use in armoured vehicles was produced without a buttstock. (Johnston & Nelson 2010: 409).

The Spanish decision to adopt the Modelo 1958 rifle chambered for the reduced-power cartridge proved a mistake as the version of the MG 42 machine gun adopted by the Spanish armed forces took the standard 7.62×51mm NATO cartridge. Deliveries of the Modelo 1958 began on 18 February 1958, with examples chambered for the reduced-power cartridge remaining in use until 1971, when all Spanish CETME rifles were modified, as the Modelo 1958-64-C, to take the 7.62×51mm NATO round (Johnston & Nelson 2010: 409). The CETME Model C used wooden handguards and was chambered for the 7.62×51mm NATO cartridge; it became standard with all Spanish armed forces by 1974. The CETME Model C also incorporated a flash hider designed to launch NATO-standard rifle grenades (Popenker &Williams 2004: 141).

West German testing continues

The measured progress towards adoption of the CETME rifle in West Germany was at least partially the result of HK's continued willingness to

ABOVE LEFT
A Spanish soldier armed with a CETME Model C guards the Alta Velocidad Española high-speed rail system in April 2006. (Rafa Samano/Cover/Getty Images)

ABOVE RIGHT
Pictured in January 2000 at Melilla, Spain, this member of the Spanish Legion (formerly the Spanish Foreign Legion) is armed with the CETME Model L, a 5.56×45mm rifle similar to the HK33. The Model L replaced the Model C in Spanish service from 1987, being replaced in turn by the G36 from the late 1990s. (Cesar Lucas Abreu/Cover/Getty Images)

address changes requested by West German military officials. One legacy of the G4 trials was the desire for a lightened CETME, but the reduction in weight led to more difficulty controlling the rifle during full-auto fire and, as the weight of the breechblock had also been reduced, increased the cyclic rate. The greater stress engendered by the higher rate of fire also required the use of higher-grade alloy steel for the receiver, thus increasing manufacturing costs. Concerns arose over whether the roller-delayed blowback action was truly locked upon ignition of the cartridge, resulting in careful measurement to assure the BVM, on 19 June 1958, that the bullet had already left the barrel before the rollers opened (Stevens 2006: 221).

Testing of the latest version of the CETME incorporating all of the mandated changes took place in early July 1958, with five rifles undergoing extensive testing, including four test-firing 10,000 rounds and the fifth firing until destruction. A wide array of ammunition from various sources in various countries was used. As a result of excellent performance, the DM3 (CETME), as the rifle was then known ('DM' stood for *Deutsche Modelo*), was deemed ready for production on 10 July 1958 (Stevens 2006: 222).

Visser's involvement

It is important to understand the part that Henk Visser, the manager of the Dutch ammunition company Nederlandse Wapen en Munitiefabriek (NWM), would play in the CETME/G3 saga. Initially, NWM had approached CETME about producing 7.92×41mm ammunition for their rifle (Stevens 2006: 223). In June 1957, Visser concluded a licensing agreement that gave him the production rights for the CETME design in the Netherlands and its overseas possessions. Visser demonstrated CETME rifles to the Dutch Army and Dutch Marines, though no orders materialized. NWM attempted to gain the international production rights, but CETME was not willing to assign other foreign production rights until the rights for supplying CETMEs to West Germany had been finalized (Stevens 2006: 223).

Visser was undeterred and produced a brochure in Spanish, German and English touting NWM as the sole representatives of CETME (Stevens 2006: 224). HK took exception to claims in the brochure that the 'weapon needs no special facilities for its manufacture except for the barrel, and can be manufactured by farming out orders for various parts to any small industry in the country' (quoted in Stevens 2006: 225). HK was, of course, well aware that the CETME rifle required skilled workers and engineers, as well as specialized equipment for manufacture. Visser was also involved in the production of trials rifles by HK in October 1957, for Finland: these were chambered for the 7.62×39mm round and took magazines that were similar to those of the AK-47 assault rifle but were not interchangeable. Only two or three rifles were produced as prototypes, but these never even made it to Finland for trials (Stevens 2006: 227–28). In the early 1960s Finland would adopt the excellent 7.62×39mm RK 62 assault rifle, which took AK-47 magazines and was produced in Finland by Valmet.

HK G3 prototype with a pressed-wood stock and scope rails stamped into the top of the receiver. (Collector Grade Publications)

As an effective representative of NWM, Visser managed to arrange demonstrations for various South American armies in Ecuador, as well as in the Dominican Republic. NWM never set up production facilities in the Netherlands, but did order a small number of rifles from CETME and HK with NWM markings.

Visser arranged to buy a disused US factory for the production of .60-calibre ammunition at a nominal price, according to Stevens as thanks for developing the 7.62mm NATO blank cartridge for the US armed forces. The machinery was easily converted to produce the 20×102mm round for the M61 Vulcan rotary cannon (Stevens 2006: 231). The story after that becomes somewhat convoluted, but because of Visser's involvement with CETME and HK and his previous distribution agreement, it proved desirable for him to give up all claim for producing the G3 rifle once it was adopted by West Germany. The BVM especially wanted Visser to cede his claim to worldwide production rights. After agreeing to waive any claim to production rights, NWM received a 20-year contract to produce one-third of all the 20mm ammunition for the Bundeswehr. As NWM did not really have the production capacity to manufacture CETME/G3 rifles, the deal proved satisfactory for both Visser and the West German government (Johnston & Nelson 2010: 402).

During 1958, the Spanish government prepared for production of CETME rifles to begin at factories in La Coruña and Oviedo; later, production would be transferred to Santa Bárbara de Industrias Militares SA. During this period, CETME produced 20,000 rifles for the Spanish Army, while training workmen from the two factories that would be producing the rifle in the future. CETME also rendered assistance in preparing the tooling needed to produce the rifles. The CETME Modelo 1958 that would be produced for the Spanish armed forces incorporated some of the changes specified by the West Germans as well

This is one of the prototype CETME rifles in 7.62×39mm calibre made up by HK for Finnish trials. Instead of this rifle, the Finns would adopt the 7.62×39mm RK 62 assault rifle, a Finnish copy derivative of the AK-47. (© Royal Armouries PR.11213)

THE G3 EXPOSED

7.62×51mm G3A3 battle rifle

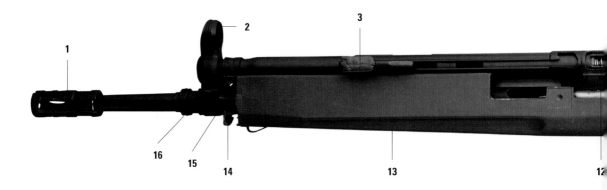

This sectionalized G3 instructional model shows operating features for instructing troops in the use of the rifle. The model would also be useful for armourers as it allows study of the operating parts *in situ*. (© Royal Armouries PR.12150)

1. Flash hider
2. Front sight and front-sight shroud
3. Cocking handle
4. Diopter rear sight
5. Buffer
6. Support for buffer housing/buffer screw, self-locking
7. Rear sling-mounting point
8. Stowage for buttstock locking pins
9. Butt
10. Stock
11. Magazine body
12. Recoil spring
13. Handguard
14. Stud
15. Eyebolt, front sling-attachment point
16. Grenade-launcher ring
17. Locking piece
18. Bolt carrier/bolt body
19. Buttstock locking pins
20. Selector switch
21. Pistol grip
22. Trigger guard
23. Trigger
24. Trigger pack
25. Magazine release
26. Magazine spring
27. Bolt head

23

THE HK33

According to Johnston & Nelson, the HK32, as the scaled-down G3 chambered for the 7.62×39mm cartridge and intended for trials by the Finns was designated, provided the basis for the HK33 (Johnston & Nelson 2010: 432). Designed by Tilo Möller, who would later head research and development at HK and was the primary designer of the MP5 submachine gun (Stevens 2006: 319), the HK33 was HK's bid to compete against the US M16 by offering an HK roller-delayed blowback design that was ergonomically similar to the G3, but chambered for the 5.56×45mm cartridge. The smaller cartridge allowed the HK33 to take a 25-round magazine, as opposed to the 20-round magazine that was standard for the G3; 40-round magazines were also available. Designed for export, the HK33 was produced from 1968; it was marketed in the United States through Harrington & Richardson as the H&R T223 (Stevens 2006: 319). A small number of T223 rifles were purchased by the US Navy and used by the SEALs in Vietnam.

A carbine version of the HK33 was developed as the HK33K, but the even more compact HK53 SMG, firing the 5.56×45mm cartridge from a 25-round magazine, proved to be an outstanding special-forces weapon. According to Johnston & Nelson, the HK53 was altered so that a canvas bag could be fitted to catch the brass cases when the weapon was fired from within a vehicle and a special receiver end cap was fitted to replace the buttstock; this version of the HK53 was originally designated the MICV Supplemental Weapon (MICV: mechanized infantry combat vehicle). In its final incarnation, which also included a quick-change barrel with lugs that locked into the ball mount of an armoured vehicle and a rear cocking handle, it was designated the MICV SW Firing Port Weapon (Johnston & Nelson 2010: 439).

A close-up of the stock, pistol grip and trigger of the HK53. It proved especially popular with British special forces. (Author)

as some resulting from the Spanish trials. At this point, the Modelo 1958 was chambered for the 7.62×51mm 'light' round (Johnston & Nelson 2010: 412).

A final agreement on adoption of the CETME/G3 by West Germany still had to be reached. Complicating the issue was the insistence by Rheinmetall that the CETME design infringed on World War Grossfuss patents acquired by Rheinmetall. (These patents referred to the MG 42 machine gun and were possibly related to the *Grossfuss Sturmgewehr* that had been designed by Kurt Horn.) Because of delays in reaching an agreement on production of the rifle in West Germany, in June 1957, CETME warned HK and Rheinmetall that if an agreement on production rights could not be reached, CETME would offer the production rights to the BVM (Johnston & Nelson 2010: 413).

Negotiations continued between the West Germans and Spanish until 19 March 1958, when the West Germans let the Spanish know that negotiations to produce the CETME in West Germany were on hold while it was determined whether or not the Bundeswehr would order additional FN FAL rifles to promote standardization with other NATO countries (Johnston & Nelson 2010: 413). The possibility that West Germany might not adopt the CETME design was a rude awakening for the Spanish, who countered by offering a contract to the BMV that now included export rights for HK and Rheinmetall. Suitably satisfied, the West Germans gave CETME a provisional contract on 3 June 1958. Initial contracts were signed between the two countries on 4 February

1959; even so, the final contract granting the West Germans the right to develop and produce the CETME as the G3 rifle was not agreed until 5 March 1962. The primary reason for this delay was Spanish reservations about HK being able to develop the rifle further and sell it to other countries without CETME's agreement (Johnston & Nelson 2010: 414).

HK begins G3 production

The protracted negotiations did not prevent HK from beginning G3 production, as a contract was granted to produce 150,000 of the rifles for the Bundeswehr on 30 January 1959 (Stevens 2006: 235). Drawing upon an HK report titled *Kurze Darstellung der Entwicklung des Gewehres G3 anhand von verschiedenen Modellan* ('A Short Representation of the Development of the Various Models of the G3 Rifle'), Stevens notes that these early rifles each weighed 3.9kg (without magazine and sling); they omitted the bipod and carrying handle and were fitted with a sheet-metal handguard and 20-round steel magazine; the folding rear peep-sight had two positions (200m and 300m) and the conical front sight could be adjusted vertically and laterally; and a scope could be mounted on every rifle if desired (Stevens 2006: 235). Presumably this last feature refers to the ability to mount the scope by clamping it to the integral receiver rails. The type of mount would evolve, but the basic mounting system would remain the same for later-production rifles.

The first 200 rifles of the initial G3 contract were delivered in September 1959; the 150,000 rifles had all been delivered by August 1962 (Stevens 2006: 237). Relatively early in the production, during 1960, the distinctive HK diopter rear sight that would become closely identified with the G3 and later HK weapons was introduced (Stevens 2006: 241–42). Also during 1960, experimentation with various types of retractable stock for the G3 rifles to be issued to airborne and armoured troops was carried out, resulting in the distinctive stock of the G3A4. Yet another innovation, included in G3 production by March 1961, was the flash hider/grenade launcher (Stevens 2006: 244).

An HK G3 shown disassembled into primary components, 1961, showing the hooded front sight and black plastic pistol grip. (Courtesy US National Park Service, Springfield Armory National Historic Site, 019-058-66/ORD-61)

A right-side view of an HK G3, 1961. In Bundeswehr service, G3 variants were given Bundeswehr designations. Variants included the G3A1, with a wooden handguard and retractable stock, adopted in October 1963; the G3A2, with plastic furniture (tropical handguard), adopted in June 1962; the G3A3, with plastic furniture and the *Freischwinger* (FS) handguard, adopted in December 1964; the G3A4, which was the G3A3 with a retractable stock, adopted in December 1964; and the G3A3ZF, with a telescopic sight, adopted in December 1964 (Stevens 2006: 259). Other designations that might be encountered include the G3TGS, a version fitted with the HK79 underbarrel grenade launcher. (Courtesy US National Park Service, Springfield Armory National Historic Site, 019-058-64/ORD-61)

IMPROVING THE G3

Initially, there were some durability problems with the G3 in actual service, which resulted in the FN FAL (G1) staying in West German service until at least the mid-1960s. Nevertheless, production continued along with the incorporation of various improvements. An order for an additional 100,000 rifles was placed with HK on 9 November 1962; these would be delivered by August 1963 (Stevens 2006: 247).

Drawing upon the same HK report mentioned earlier, Stevens lists the characteristics of the 1962-production G3 rifles (Stevens 2006: 248). He notes that the weight rose to 4kg (without magazine and sling) and that the rifles had the following features: slotted flash hider; wooden handguard; bent safety lever offering improved operation; reinforced cocking-handle tube; and a rotary rear sight with four positions (100m–400m), the 100m position being an open notch for rapid fire.

A feature that should be mentioned is the rollers that were so critical to the G3's operation. These were manufactured of *Schnellarbeitsstahl* ('high-speed steel'), a 4140 type of alloy with outside nitriding to add carbon to the surface of the tough inner core. These rollers were hardened to Rockwell C 63+4, a high degree of hardness. Although various sizes of rollers were available for fitting during early prototype production, once mass production began, only three sizes of rollers were produced – the standard size and two oversized that could be used to correct headspace in rifles that had seen substantial use (Stevens 2006: 283). Using a gauge, 'headspace' (bolt gap) is correct when the gap between bolt head and bolt-head carrier is between 0.1mm and 0.5mm. If it is greater, the +2 (8.02mm) rollers, identified by a single bar on top, or the +4 (8.04mm) rollers, identified by two bars on top, would be substituted for the standard 8.00mm rollers.

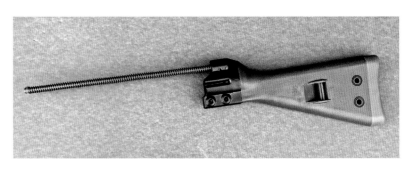

An HK stock in green removed from the receiver and showing the recoil spring and guide rod. (Author)

A G3A1 with collapsible stock, slotted flash hider, wooden handguard and aluminium magazine, *c.*1962. Note the lever located just in front of the butt to release the stock for extension. (Collector Grade Publications)

G3 RIFLE PRODUCTION AT HK

HK continued fulfilling new G3 contracts for the Bundeswehr until 1969, at which point sufficient rifles were on hand for conceivable future needs. Prior to the German adoption of the G36 in 1997, many of the G3 rifles in service were returned to HK for refurbishment.

An interesting film showing G3 production at HK, made by the Bundeswehr in the 1970s, offers some insights into the rifle as delivered to the Bundeswehr. Apparently, all parts were manufactured in-house at HK, thus eliminating any potential problems with subcontractors. It was also apparent that rigorous quality-control measures were in place, including test-firing each rifle from a machine rest. Reportedly, accuracy was held to 3 MOA (3in or 7.6cm) at 100m. A final point of note in the film is that it is apparent from the relatively few manufacturing steps that the engineers who developed the CETME and the G3 were successful in developing a technically advanced rifle that could be manufactured relatively simply in terms of time and cost.

As a result of the agreement with respect to the Grossfuss patents, Rheinmetall also produced G3 rifles. Even so, Rheinmetall was only a production facility and had to follow HK's lead on any design changes. Nevertheless, according to Stevens, Rheinmetall manufactured a total of 500,000 G3 rifles, reaching peak production during the 1960s of 8,000 units per month (Stevens 2006: 287).

Rheinmetall ceased producing the G3 during the bidding period for a new Bundeswehr contract for G3 rifles and MG3 machine guns. In fact, according to Johnston & Nelson, the first 400,000 G3s produced by HK were of poor quality and were withdrawn from service and destroyed as soon as replacements were available. Virtually all of the G3s produced by Rheinmetall were also destroyed due to poor quality. This helps to explain the difficulty in reconciling the actual number of G3s produced for the Bundeswehr (Johnston & Nelson 2010: 416).

As the MG3 was based on the MG 42 machine gun developed by Rheinmetall, that firm kept a monopoly on supplying the Bundeswehr with the MG3. To gain leverage against Rheinmetall, HK threatened to bid for the new MG3 contract, a weapon HK could likely produce less expensively than Rheinmetall, the prices of which were based on the older firm's monopoly. A compromise was reached in which HK would, henceforth, produce all of the G3s for the Bundeswehr, while Rheinmetall would produce all of the MG3 machine guns (Stevens 2006: 292).

After deliveries against the contracts for the Bundeswehr were complete, HK continued to produce the G3 until 2001. One major change occurred during 1986 when G3s produced by HK began using a plastic moulding that combines the pistol grip, trigger guard and lower receiver into one unit (Gangarosa 2001: 75).

This G3A3 has the green furniture that became standard for Bundeswehr G3 rifles after 1964. This example may have been produced for export, as it has the wider type of handguard. As is evident here, the standard selector switch for the G3 is marked 'S' (*Sicher* – safe), 'E' (*Einzelfeuer* – single shot), and 'F' (*Feuerstoss* – burst fire). (© Royal Armouries PR.1033)

Exterior and interior views of the more compact and lighter tropical handguard preferred by many for use on the G3. The interior view shows the heat shield that helps dissipate heat build-up during full-auto fire. (Author)

One other important change would occur before the G3 reached the form that would become standard until the 1980s. In 1964, polymer furniture was adopted to replace the wood, which had been produced for HK in Italy. Originally, HK considered black furniture, but the Bundeswehr wanted G3s with olive-green furniture. For the Bundeswehr, olive-green furniture became standard in 1964, while black polymer furniture was available for export orders. Late in 1964, the plastic handguard was redesigned as the *Freischwinger* (FS: 'cantilevered'). This handguard eliminated the transverse pin previously used. The transverse pin had passed between the charging tube and the barrel, thus applying pressure on parts and possibly adversely affecting accuracy. The new handguard used a sheet-metal clip that prevented the pin or handguard from touching the barrel (Stevens 2006: 252).

Later, two variations of handguard were made available for the G3: a slimmer design known as the 'tropical handguard' and a wider 'beavertail' type designed to accept a quick-detach bipod (Johnston & Nelson 2010: 424).

An assortment of 20-round G3 aluminium magazines made by (left to right) HK, Kongsberg (Norway) and Rheinmetall. Although 30-round box magazines and 50-round drum magazines are also available for the G3, they are not frequently encountered. When original-production high-capacity magazines in good condition are encountered they bring a premium, especially the HK G8 drum, which can sell for over US$1,000. (Author)

USE
The G3 in action

The G3 ranks with the AK-47, M16 and FN FAL as one of the most widely used weapons of the Cold War. At least 80 countries acquired the G3 either as a standard service rifle or for specialist usage, and at least a dozen countries have produced copies of the G3. For comparison, the FN FAL was also used by at least 80 countries, while the AK-47 has been used by well over 100 countries, as well as various insurgent groups.

The largest combat usage of the G3 occurred during the Iran–Iraq War (1980–88), as it was the principal service rifle of Iran. It has seen far more use in the hands of insurgents and government troops during various counter-insurgency campaigns. These have included fighting in Portuguese Africa, Rhodesia, Nigeria, South Africa, Northern Ireland, Iran, Lebanon, Nicaragua, El Salvador, Turkey, Ethiopia, Yugoslavia, Sierra Leone, Bangladesh, Pakistan, Afghanistan, Colombia, Mexico, Syria, Somalia, Iraq and Yemen.

Pictured in October 1995, German motorized infantry of Jäger Regiment 57 aim their G3A3s from within a truck. Although the G3 is compact enough for employment from within a truck, its length with the fixed stock would make it more difficult to deploy from within an armoured personnel carrier. A noteworthy variant of the G3 is the G3KA4, a compact version with a 315mm barrel and a retractable stock. Normally, a short-barrelled carbine of this type that uses a gas-operated system has functioning issues with a shorter barrel, but the G3's roller-delayed blowback system allows the shorter-barrelled version to function reliably (Gangarosa 2001: 73). (Melde Bildagentur/ullstein bild via Getty Images)

THE G3 IN COLD-WAR AFRICA

An interesting though limited use of the CETME rifle took place during the counter-insurgency war in Algeria (1954–62). In March 1961, the Danish freighter *Margot Hansen* was stopped by a French naval patrol off the coast of Algeria. Aboard the freighter were contraband arms and 7.62×51mm ammunition intended for the Armée de Libération Nationale (ANL) and Front de Libération Nationale (FLN). The confiscated weapons were placed into a French Navy arsenal where seized arms were normally stored. Included were 200 CETME Model B rifles, which offered more firepower than the 7.5×54mm MAS 49/56 semi-automatic rifles the French were using. The only problem was that the CETME rifles lacked their firing pins. As the French personnel felt that the confiscated rifles, offering 20-round magazine capacity and select fire, would give them a substantial boost in firepower over the MAS 49/56, which offered semi-auto fire only and a magazine capacity of ten rounds, they requested that the captured rifles be issued to them. Apparently, the CETME Model Bs were used primarily as light machine guns by the French (Stevens 2006: 422–23).

The French Navy arsenal attempted to manufacture replacement firing pins for the CETME Model B rifles, but the result was not very satisfactory, as the firing pins had a tendency to break frequently. As a result, personnel of the Commandos Marine using the CETMEs went into action carrying spare firing pins. The captured ammunition also proved to be of poor quality, apparently assembled from rejected components. After encountering reliability problems with the captured ammunition, the Commandos Marine switched to French-manufactured ammunition, which was reliable. The CETME Model B rifles remained in operational service with the Commandos Marine until at least 1978 and continued in limited use into the 1990s, when all but a few retained for museums were destroyed (Stevens 2006: 426–27).

One thing that is not clear is why the French could not order firing pins from CETME, either overtly or covertly through the Service de Documentation Extérieure et de Contre-Espionnage (SDECE), the French overseas intelligence agency. The most likely explanation is that the use of captured CETMEs by the Commandos Marine was not considered a high-enough priority to merit the effort.

Portugal's colonial war in Africa (1961–74) saw the G3's first sustained use in harsh conditions. Although the G3 was used by all of the Portuguese units serving in Mozambique and Angola, its use with the elite light-infantry units is most illustrative, as they saw the most combat. Portuguese operations involved riverine and land patrols, conducted to establish a presence in the region. Beginning in March 1963, Portuguese *Fuzileiros* (Marines) used launches for mobile operations on the Zaire (aka Congo) River, especially launching patrols along the river banks in rubber boats. To give the crews sufficient firepower to gain superiority over any insurgents, the G3 – presumably the version made under licence in Portugal as the m/961 – proved an important weapon, replacing the 9×19mm FBP m/948 submachine gun and serving alongside MG 42 and Oerlikon machine guns (Cann 2016: 27).

While patrolling along the banks of the Zaire River, the *Fuzileiros* carried m/961 rifles equipped to launch grenades and also bazookas (Cann 2016: 42). Though operating in relatively small patrols, the *Fuzileiros* were well equipped to gain fire superiority over any insurgents they encountered, the bazookas and G3s with grenade launchers giving a direct and indirect fire stand-off capability.

Another Portuguese counter-insurgency unit, the *Flechas* (Arrows), which recruited among former insurgents and other Africans, found that the G3 was not suited to all of its troops. The *Flechas* were special-forces units formed by the Portuguese Polícia Internacional e de Defesa do Estado (PIDE: International Police and State Defence), a state security police agency renamed the Direcçcão-Geral de Segurança (DGS: Directorate-General of Security) in 1968. They operated in Angola and Mozambique, often on patrols or tracking operations, and were also used on pseudo-guerrilla operations to trap insurgents. In many ways their missions were similar to those conducted by the more famous Selous Scouts in Rhodesia. *Flecha* units varied in size but usually comprised around 30 men. They were armed with a mix of Portuguese weapons and captured insurgent firearms, though some retained their traditional bows and arrows.

The m/961 was used by the *Flechas*, but its length (1,026mm) made it harder to handle by smaller-statured indigenous personnel, who often preferred the shorter AK-47 (871mm) despite the Soviet weapon being 0.68kg heavier than the m/961. By the mid-1970s, the longer but lighter M16 assault rifle (1,003mm, 3.27kg) was fielded (Cann 2013: 34).

ABOVE LEFT
Portuguese commandos training at Maputo in July 1973, during the Mozambique counter-insurgency campaign. G3 rifles for Portuguese forces were produced under licence by Fábrica de Braço de Prata in G3A3 and G3A4 versions. As would seem logical for campaigning in Africa, these rifles have the tropical handguard. (AFP/Getty Images)

ABOVE RIGHT
A Portuguese colonial soldier in Mozambique during July 1973; the magazine in the rifle is the lightweight alloy one often issued to paratroopers and commandos. (David Hume Kennerly/Getty Images)

January 1979: Rhodesian 'Spear of the People' local security force members are being trained with G3 rifles likely acquired from the Portuguese. (Keystone/Hulton Archive/Getty Images)

The Rhodesians also faced a counter-insurgency war on the borders of Portuguese colonial possessions, which resulted in some shared intelligence and military exchanges. Facing an embargo on arms imports, the Rhodesians found that the m/961 was one of the few battle rifles they could acquire, though sometimes it took devious means to do so. Reportedly, many of the m/961s used in Rhodesia were obtained via an auction in Lisbon late in 1975. According to Hamilton Spence, formerly managing director of Interarms UK, these rifles were purchased by South Africa. Some were reportedly supplied to the mercenary leader Mike Hoare for his failed November 1981 *coup d'état* attempt in the Seychelles, while others were supplied to Rhodesia, as was proven by the serial numbers of some of the rifles used in Rhodesia (Brogan & Zarca 1983: 166–70).

Rhodesian forces had familiarity with the m/961 prior to receiving substantial numbers of the rifles through cooperation along the Rhodesia/ Mozambique border against Frente de Libertação de Moçambique (FRELIMO) guerrillas. Rhodesian tracking teams, led by Major Rob Southey and Captain Ron Reid-Daly (later to lead the Selous Scouts), had a generally good opinion of the Portuguese troops. Alex Binda, who praised the reliability of the m/961, noted that on patrol the Portuguese carried the m/961 by grasping the barrel and resting it on the shoulder, whereas the Rhodesian trackers heading the patrol would hold their

The G3 in Rhodesian service (opposite)

Two Rhodesian soldiers of Grey's Scouts with their G3 rifles. Firing a rifle from horseback, especially the G3 with its noticeable recoil, took discipline and practice. It also meant training the horse not to shy away from gunfire. Normally, mounted troops were trained not to fire their weapons directly alongside the animal's ears. One trooper is engaging while the other searches for a target.

The G3 saw service right across Africa during the Cold War years. Pictured in September 1989, this Kenyan anti-poaching patrol includes personnel armed with G3 rifles; poachers are often heavily armed and so to defend wildlife and themselves, game rangers must also be well armed. (William F. Campbell/The LIFE Images Collection/Getty Images)

weapons at the ready. It is interesting that Binda, who was admittedly a member of the Rhodesian Army Pay Corps rather than a combat soldier and was chosen for his language skills, mentions the Portuguese carrying their rifles over their shoulders in a non-ready position, while the Rhodesians had theirs ready for action. It should be noted, however, that photos exist showing highly trained Rhodesian soldiers carrying their rifles in the same manner if combat did not seem imminent.

Eventually, G3s would be widely used alongside the FN FAL and captured AK-47s by various units in the Rhodesian Security Forces, including the Selous Scouts and Grey's Scouts, a mounted infantry unit. Members of the Rhodesian Guard Force, which was assigned to provide security for Protected Villages, were initially issued with .303 Lee-Enfield bolt-action rifles, which were later replaced by badly worn FN FAL rifles. Eventually, however, the Guard Force received new G3 rifles.

Generally, based on the accounts of veterans of the conflict in Rhodesia, troops thought more highly of the FAL than the G3. David Tomkins, who appeared in many war zones and participated in various conflicts, found himself in Rhodesia early in 1979. Tomkins stayed with a friend who was an armourer for the Rhodesian Ministry of Internal Affairs, and recalled that the pressure of international sanctions on the Rhodesian regime meant that damaged weapons – including G3 and FAL rifles – were repaired rather than being scrapped. Damaged rifle barrels were shortened and the breechblocks modified so the operating system still functioned (Tomkins 2008: 188). The G3, with its roller-delayed blowback action, was less dependent on gas than the FAL. Nevertheless, shortening the barrel of the G3 substantially may have required some alterations to the operating system.

THE G3 IN CENTRAL AND SOUTH AMERICA

The armed forces of Central and South American countries have often fielded an array of weapons in accordance with their dependence on foreign aid or other factors influencing the acquisition process. German rifles have traditionally been popular in South America, with widespread adoption of the G3 for at least limited usage. Brigada Especial Operativa Halcón, the Buenos Aires Police Hawk Special-Operations Brigade, has used the G3, but the primary Argentine battle rifle has been the licence-produced FAL, as used in the Falklands War in 1982; more recently, the US M4 has been widely used by the Argentine armed forces.

As well as government forces, the G3 has also equipped irregulars fighting in the various insurgencies across the region. In the summer of 1988, David Tomkins became involved in a scheme to raise a mercenary force to operate against Fuerzas Armadas Revolucionarias de Colombia (FARC) guerrillas in Colombia. The mission included striking against FARC leadership and supply lines. The operation was privately financed and without official approval of the Colombian government, which had been weak in countering the FARC threat. The G3 rifle – most likely copies made in Colombia by Industria Militar de Colombia (Indumil) – would play an important part in the mercenaries' plans, but the initial batch of six G3s were a disappointment; more were delivered later. Tomkins notes that he and his associates were very familiar with the rifle, but conducted extensive training with it all the same, although live firing was limited as it would have alarmed the local population (Tomkins 2008: 262).

As with many operations of this type, time passed with little being accomplished, though Tomkins and the men he had recruited eventually did train some local counter-guerrillas. Although it appears possible that counter-guerrillas trained by Tomkins and his associates had some success in countering local narco-terrorists, they do not appear to have had great success against FARC.

These members of Ecuador's Cuerpo de Infanteria de Marina (Naval Infantry Corps aka Marines) are armed with the HK33A2 rifle. (PH2 John D. Bivera/Wikimedia/Public Domain)

Today, Bolivia, Chile, Colombia and Peru are listed as former users of the G3, but now have M4/M16, AK-47, Galil and other rifles in their armouries instead. Mexico has used the G3 as its standard rifle alongside the HK33, with both rifles being licensed and locally produced; even so, some Mexican special units use the M4 carbine. Paraguay, where German influence has been strong for decades, has used the G3 but also the FAL, the Taiwanese T65 and the M4; the G3 is now in reserve.

A US Marine armed with an M16 (at left) and a Chilean Marine armed with an HK53 (at right) carrying out joint training. (US Navy/Wikimedia/Public Domain)

G3 BAYONETS

Many of the bayonets supplied for the G3 were produced by Eickhorn of Solingen, a well-known German manufacturer of high-quality blades. By changing the bayonet adaptor, Eickhorn bayonets could be modified to fit a wide array of NATO service rifles. A variety of adaptors allowed other bayonets to be affixed to the G3. For example, one adaptor allowed the US M7 bayonet to be affixed. Later G3 bayonets no longer needed a bayonet adaptor, instead affixing directly to the rifle's cocking tube.

The basic G3 bayonet was adopted in 1959 by the Bundeswehr along with the G3 rifle. The bayonet was approximately 305mm overall length and had a 165mm blade and 22mm muzzle ring. The blade was similar to that of the US M3 trench knife or M1 Carbine bayonet. The grips are one-piece, plastic ribbed and 'bellied' with a flash-guard behind the muzzle ring to protect the plastic grip from scorching when the rifle is fired.

Eickhorn also made the KCB-70 M1 bayonet that was originally designed for the Stoner 63A1 assault rifle. This wire-cutter design was also produced for the G3 rifle. In addition to the hole in the blade to engage a lug on the scabbard for wire-cutting, the blade has saw teeth. For wire-cutting, the bayonet/scabbard works in a manner similar to the AKM or US M9 bayonet.

Among other variants of the G3 bayonet are those from the following countries: Denmark, Greece, Iran, Norway, Pakistan, Spain, Sweden and Turkey. Some of the other countries that adopted the G3 seem to have used standard Eickhorn G3 bayonets, while others used M7-type bayonets. Among those with distinctive differences were those used by Pakistan (produced with a bowie-point blade of British No. 5 bayonet style) and Turkey (with a longer blade than the standard G3 bayonet – 241mm rather than 165mm). Rarely encountered is a G3 bayonet that was produced by Rheinmetall when that firm began producing the G3 rifle in the mid-1960s. It has a longer blade than the HK/Eickhorn type – 238mm – a less bulbous grip and a different-shaped pommel.

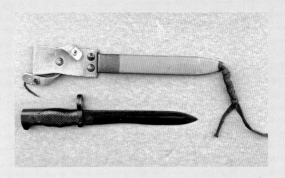

The CETME M1964 bayonet used by Spanish forces has chequered plastic grips and a bolo-shaped blade. A variant of this blade was made for export to Guatemala in 1969. When Spain adopted the 5.56×45mm version of the CETME rifle in the late 1980s, it also adopted a new bayonet – the Model L – patterned to some extent after the US M4 bayonet-knife. (Author)

A standard HK-produced G3 bayonet. To affix a bayonet to the G3 rifle, the circular-sectioned lug on the rear of the bayonet pommel must be pushed onto the bayonet adaptor until a catch on the bayonet engages an interior depression through one side of the adaptor. When the catch on the bayonet is released, the adaptor spring pushes the bayonet out of its fixed position. This is different from most bayonets, which must be removed manually. (Author)

Greek sailors armed with G3A3s take part in a Greek Independence Day parade on 25 March 2016. Unlike the typical bayonet, those for HK rifles attach above rather than below the barrel in an inverted position. When grasped with the muzzle ring forward of the knuckles, the standard HK bayonet is in a normal position for close combat or utility blade use. (ARIS MESSINIS/ AFP/Getty Images)

THE IRAN–IRAQ WAR

The G3 was adopted as the primary Iranian issue rifle while the Shah was still in power. The rifle has been produced under licence by Defense Industries Organization as the G3A6, with those manufactured during the Shah's reign marked with the Pahlavi Lion. Reportedly, after the fall of the Shah in 1979, the quality of G3A6 production declined and production dropped as low as 500 per month at one point. During the Iranian Revolution of 1979, at least some of the revolutionaries were armed with M1 Garand rifles stolen from armouries.

The Iran–Iraq War of 1980–88 involved hundreds of thousands of Iranian troops who were primarily armed with G3s produced at the Mosalsalsasi Weapons Factory, which suffered damage during the conflict; the G3 saw a great deal of combat (Jones 2007: 173). The M1 Garand, which had been used in Iran prior to the adoption of the G3, saw some use with Iranian rear-area security forces. During the conflict, the G3A6 was the principal Iranian rifle, though the AK-47 was also widely used. The G3 will definitely allow effective engagement at greater range than the AK-47 – assuming, that is, the soldier firing the G3 is well trained and motivated. The fact that the Iranians could field few tanks and other armoured vehicles required them to emphasize infantry combat, but few accounts are available in English that describe the soldiers' experiences with the G3 rifle.

Various factors during the Iran–Iraq War should have favoured the G3 rifle over the Iraqi AK-47. Despite a front stretching 1,175km from the Turkish border to the Persian Gulf, only the *c*.400km sector between Mandali, Iraq, and Bostan, Iran, lent itself to mobile warfare using armour and artillery in conjunction with air support. Iraqi troops, better trained in combined-arms operations, proved superior to the Iranians in this sector. The lighter, more compact AK-47, more controllable in full-auto fire, in the hands of Iraqi troops had an advantage in these types of operations and the Iraqis were generally victorious.

In the north, the 515km front from Oshnovīyeh, Iran, to Khanaqin, Iraq, was mountainous terrain which rendered Iraq's superiority in

Pictured in October 1980, these Iranian Revolutionary Guards near Qasr-e Shirin, Iran, are armed with G3 rifles. (Kaveh Kazemi/ Getty Images)

Iranian women train with the G3 in a camp near Iran, October 1986. It is noteworthy that the rifles are equipped with the slim (tropical) handguard, which may be a concession to the women's smaller hands. (Mohsen Shandiz/ Sygma via Getty Images)

armour, artillery and air power less important there. Mountainous terrain offers a tactical advantage to longer-ranged, more powerful rifles, however, and here Iranian infantry had an advantage in that the G3 rifle allowed them to engage at ranges where the AK-47 was less effective. It was not until 1988, however, that the Iranians made substantial gains in this area of the conflict.

For the early years of the war, Iran's major offensives were along the 260km-wide southern sector from Bostan in the north to the Persian Gulf. This terrain was flat and open, so the longer-ranging G3 would have conferred an advantage on the Iranians, while the Iraqi use of armour was limited due to the presence of damp, marshy areas. The terrain also favoured the Iranian use of small groups of infiltrators, thus requiring the Iraqis to devote resources to clearing them out. Once again, the more powerful, longer-ranged G3 was an advantage, though if it came to close combat the handier AK-47 may have had the upper hand when used in full-auto fire during an assault. If close combat ensued, both the G3 and AK-47 were equipped with bayonets. Subjectively, I would say that the AK-47 bayonet would lend itself better to slashing in close combat.

Despite having three times the manpower of the Iraqis, the Iranians could not break the stalemate. Their inability to produce enough G3A6 rifles to arm their army necessitated the acquisition of AK-47 rifles of

The G3 in the Iran–Iraq War (overleaf)

Iranian troops during the Iran–Iraq War shelter behind a knocked-out tank to engage Iraqi troops. The Iranian troops are armed with the Iranian-manufactured version of the G3. As they are taking part in an assault, the Iranians have their bayonets, which are different from standard German G3 bayonets, mounted. The Iraqis are armed with the AK-47 assault rifle. The 7.62×51mm G3 would normally give an advantage in range and penetration over the 7.62×39mm AK-47, though at this distance, longer range would have little advantage.

An Iranian man armed with a G3 stands watch at the funeral of Ayatollah Khomeini, 8 June 1989. (Régis BOSSU/Sygma via Getty Images)

various types, thus mitigating the advantages the G3 bestowed on the Iranians during combat with the AK-47-equipped Iraqis.

Within Iranian infantry forces today are elite light-infantry commandos who are typically armed with AK-47 rifles, although the standard weapon in use in the Iranian Army continues to be the G3. However, members of the 23rd Takavar (Commando) Division, one of the Iranian Army's most prestigious units and one that saw extensive combat in the Iran–Iraq War, are reportedly armed with newly manufactured G3 rifles with collapsible stocks. Some reports designate this unit as an airborne-rapid-deployment force.

Though the G3A6 remains in service, Iran has developed newer weapons including the KH-2002, a 5.56×45mm 'bullpup' design based on the Chinese Norinco CQ. (The term 'bullpup' refers to a rifle with the action and magazine behind the trigger group.) Taking advantage of the range of the 7.62×51mm round, the Iranian Army now has a DMR based on the G3A6 that mounts the Ghadir-4 3–12-power scope. Iran Defence Products also offers fixed- and collapsible-stock versions of the G3 for export.

Iranian police participate in a military parade in Tehran, September 1996. Iranian G3A6 rifles are readily identified by their dark-green stock and handguard. (Scott Peterson/ Liaison)

THE G3 IN ASIA AND THE PACIFIC

South-East Asia and the Pacific

Heckler & Koch marketed the G3, the HK33 and other weapons aggressively and offered assistance in setting up facilities for licensed production. The saga of the adoption and use of the G3 and later the HK33 in Burma (since 1989, known as Myanmar) offers an excellent example.

The article 'Strong and Fast: German Arms in Burma' (Deckert 2007) offers some interesting information on the G3 and HK33 in use in Burma. According to the article, West Germany first agreed to export arms and set up ammunition production facilities in Burma to reduce the possibility that Burma, which was 'non-aligned' in the Cold War, would establish diplomatic relations with East Germany. Initial sales of the G3 were made through Fritz-Werner AG, a German firm that still specializes in machinery for the production of ammunition. Fritz-Werner, which had helped set up the Burmese ammunition factories, arranged the purchase of G3 rifles from Rheinmetall. Fritz-Werner was also the contractor that would help establish the plant in Burma for the licensed production of the G3.

In 1961, the German Foreign Office gave permission for the export of 10,000 G3 rifles to Burma, as well as four million rounds of ammunition produced by Fritz-Werner. Within the next couple of years a further 12,000 G3 rifles and 18 million rounds of ammunition were exported to Burma. Those in Germany favouring limitations on arms exports were distressed to discover that even after a large number of Burmese protestors were shot in 1988, with photographs showing HK rifles being used against the protestors, the export of machinery for ammunition production to Burma continued. The licensed production of HK weapons and ammunition took place for decades in factories set up around Rangoon by HK, the Gesellschaft für Technische Zusammenarbeit (Technical Corporation Agency) and Fritz-Werner.

The G3 was the standard military rifle of Burma from the 1960s until the 1990s. The Burmese designation for the G3 was the BA72 (Burma Army 72). Variants produced included: the BA63, a retractable-stock version; the BA100, a copy of the G3A3ZF; and a light-machine-gun version. It appears, however, that the Burmese realized that by the early 21st century Germany would no longer be willing to offer the assistance with arms and ammunition production they had previously provided. Without Germany, the Burmese turned to Israel for help in development of a 5.56×45mm weapon based on the Galil, though with some differences – the retention of the HK-type rear sight, for example. This resulted in the MA1 service rifle. The 5.56×45mm MA11 rifle retains the roller-delayed blowback action and bears many similarities to the HK33, though with some Burmese alterations. Burma has also developed the EMER K1 bullpup-type rifle, reportedly with aid from Singapore (Kenneth 2009). Some sources list the HK33 still in use in Myanmar; this presumably refers to the MA11.

In 1971, HK sold Thailand a complete factory for the licensed production of the HK33. Fritz-Werner AG had a long history with Thailand, having set up the Royal Thai Arsenal in the 1920s, and in 1975 that

company built a plant to produce 5.56×45mm ammunition in Thailand. Likewise, HK licensed production of the HK33 there. Prior to the start of production of the HK33 in Thailand, HK supplied 48,900 of the rifles to that country. Cambodian rebels were soon armed with HK33 and HK53 weapons from Thailand. There were also reports that Thailand improperly exported 3,000 HK33s to the Pinochet regime in Chile (Deckert 2008).

Elsewhere in South-East Asia and the Pacific, the G3 has seen limited use. Indonesian Air Force special forces used the G3 rifle during the counter-insurgency campaign against the Free Papua Movement in Western New Guinea (1962–present day), though the G3 has since been replaced by the M16A3 and relegated to reserve and training usage. The Papua New Guinea Defence Force has used the G3 in the past along with an array of other assault rifles, but the current standard-issue rifle is the US M16A2.

The T223 in Vietnam (opposite)

During the Vietnam War the US Navy SEALs, a relatively new special-warfare unit at the time, had substantial leeway in their choice of weapons. Among their specialities were ambushes along the waterways of the Mekong Delta. In this scene three SEALs lay down a hail of fire against Viet Cong on the river. In the foreground, the SEAL uses a Harrington & Richardson T223, a US copy of the HK33. The T223 was faster to clean and proved more reliable in the jungle than the M16, which initially experienced problems; also, 40-round magazines were available for the T223. The SEAL at right uses the Ithaca Model 37 shotgun to send swarms of 00 buckshot down range. At upper left, a third SEAL uses the Stoner 63 light machine gun with drum magazine.

The G3 in Pakistan

One of the largest military users of the G3 has been the Pakistan Army, with rifles produced by Pakistan Ordnance Factories (POF) at Wah Cantt. Figures are not available for the total number of rifles produced by POF, but as the Pakistan Army has around 1.5 million regular and reserve troops, it can be assumed that the number is significant. The POF versions of the G3 are given their own designations, with the standard G3A4 designated the G3P4, the G3A4 with shorter barrel designated the G3S, and a light version of the G3 with polymer receiver and shorter barrel designated the G3M-Tactical. Reportedly, some POF rifles were exported to Bangladesh and possibly elsewhere. Generally, POF weapons are of good quality and – based on my limited experience with the weapon – this is true of the POF G3 rifle as well. (The POF version of the HK MP5 submachine gun, with which I am much more familiar, is considered by many to be the best version of the copies and equal or close to the original HK product.)

The G3 saw combat in the hands of Pakistani troops involved in fighting against India during the Kargil Conflict of May–July 1999. Fighting broke out after Pakistani troops and Kashmiri militants crossed the Line of Control into Indian territory. The conflict ended when India recaptured territory that had been occupied by Pakistani forces. The conflict was of special interest, as it took place at high altitude in mountainous terrain, thus testing troops and equipment. The conflict caused substantial concern among the major powers, as both sides had nuclear weapons arsenals.

It is interesting to note the opinions expressed by members of Pakistan's armed forces and establishment about that country's military weapons. One point consistently made is that the G3 fires the more powerful 7.62×51mm round, while India's various assault rifles, including the Tavor TAR-21, AKM, AK-103 and M4A1/M16, fire the 5.56×45mm or 7.62×39mm cartridge. As a result, Pakistani troops enjoy an edge in terms of range during mountain combat against their Indian counterparts. Pakistani military thinking appears to be greatly influenced by the possibility of conflict with their long-time enemy, with one commentator noting that the 7.62×51mm round can penetrate Indian body armour.

Another point often mentioned in favour of the POF versions of the G3 is that they are produced in Pakistan. Respondents with infantry

This G3A2 was manufactured by Pakistan Ordnance Factories (POF) in 1974. Note the wooden stock and handguard. POF continued to manufacture the rifle with the wooden furniture until 1986, after which the G3A3 with polymer furniture was produced. (© Royal Armouries PR.5383)

A Pakistani soldier on patrol near a Shi'ite mosque in Lahore to prevent acts of sectarian violence, February 2005. His rifle is the POF-manufactured G3P4. (Paula Bronstein/Getty Images)

backgrounds note the G3's range and accuracy as well as striking power, but admit that the M4 carbine is more effective for close-quarter combat as the US weapon is handier and more controllable on full-auto. Others want to see the G3 upgraded with Picatinny rails, optics and a collapsible stock. It is also noted that when combined with the Energa rifle grenade, the G3 may be used in the anti-tank role.

At least one veteran of the Kargil Conflict fighting has pointed out that his G3 jammed frequently. As anyone trained for combat in cold climates is aware, a lack of proper lubrication is often the culprit causing malfunctions. Taking the rifle into a warm area then going back out can cause icing, as condensation collects in the heat, then freezes when exposed to cold. Proper lubrication of the G3 is particularly important due to the rifle's roller-locking system.

A Pakistani soldier stands guard in October 2010 at the bazaar in Quetta, Pakistan, amid tensions arising from US airstrikes against Afghanistan. His G3A1 rifle lacks the diopter rear sight and has a wooden handguard. (ARIF ALI/ AFP/Getty Images)

Not all Pakistani commentators favour the G3 and some point out the drawbacks of the 7.62×51mm battle rifles, criticizing the G3's weight and length and the difficulty experienced in controlling the rifle on full-auto. Others point out that, indeed, adopting a 5.56×45mm carbine might be desirable, but the cost of replacing the G3P4 and other POF rifles and setting up to produce a new calibre in quantity would be financially prohibitive in Pakistan.

Even so, members of the Pakistani military establishment are not all enamoured of the G3, and Pakistan has been interested in adopting a 5.56×45mm rifle for at least a decade. An attempt was made by POF to produce its PK-8, a 5.56×45mm G3 derivative based on the HK33K. The cost of replacing the hundreds of thousands of G3s in service, however, proved prohibitive. As a stopgap, POF provided the G3S, a carbine/paratroop version of the G3 and the G3M, which has rails for the attachment of accessories. Chinese 7.62×39mm Type 56 assault rifles were also acquired.

As of early 2016, trials were reportedly under way in Pakistan to select a new service rifle to replace the G3 and Type 56 in use by Pakistani forces. Part of the selection process will involve upgrading POF manufacturing facilities to produce the new rifle. Also to be built is a new ammunition plant. Among rifles reportedly under consideration by Pakistan are the Beretta ARX-200, CZ-806 BREN 2, FN SCAR, Kalashnikov AK-103 and Zastava M21. Any deal made by Pakistan will include the right to licence-produce the rifle in Pakistan (Ansari 2016).

It is likely that the G3 will remain in use with Pakistan's armed forces for many more years, as new rifles are produced and issued. Support troops and reserve troops are likely to retain the G3 for years, if not decades. As with other countries that have replaced their battle rifles with 5.56×45mm assault rifles, the Pakistani armed forces will likely retain scoped G3 rifles as DMRs, especially as much of the country is comprised of mountainous terrain in which the longer range of the 7.62×51mm round is desirable.

During an international defence exhibition in Karachi in November 2006, the Pakistani Prime Minister Shaukat Aziz examines a PK-8 rifle, the POF version of the HK33. It is interesting that the rifle has an Aimpoint type of red-dot optical sight mounted to make it more effective for close-quarter combat. In the foreground is the POF PK-7, a 7.62×39mm version of the G3. It appears to take AK-47 magazines; this rifle in grey is probably a mock-up rather than a functional rifle, as photos of a functional version show a blued receiver. (ASIF HASSAN/AFP/ Getty Images)

THE G3 IN EUROPE

Scandinavia and the Baltic

Evaluation of a new assault rifle for the Norwegian armed forces began in 1960 and eventually resulted in the adoption of the G3 in 1966 under the designation AG-3 (Automatgevær 3, or 'assault rifle 3'). Kongsberg Våpenfabrikk initially concluded an agreement with the Bundeswehr to produce parts for 100,000 G3 rifles as part of a repurchase agreement. Production under licence from HK began in February 1967, with 253,497 AG-3 rifles eventually being delivered to the Norwegian defence forces by November 1974.

By the mid-1990s, Norway was looking for a replacement for the AG-3. Other NATO countries had adopted rifles in 5.56×45mm NATO, and when deployed on various peacekeeping operations and to Afghanistan, Norwegian troops found most allied troops were armed with lighter 5.56×45mm rifles. Norwegian special-operations forces were using the HK G36 and the Colt Canada C8SFW by 2007, but the standard-issue rifle remained the AG-3.

By 2006, the AG-3 rifles had been in service with Norwegian forces for over 30 years and testing was undertaken to find a replacement. An upgraded version of the AG-3 was also tested alongside other candidates. Eventually, the HK416 rifle (5.56×45mm) was chosen as the standard rifle with the HK417 (7.62×51mm) selected as a DMR. Although an order was placed for 8,200 HK416 rifles in April 2007, it was decided that members of the Norwegian Home Guard would continue to use the AG-3. Rather than order the HK417, 2,500 AG-3 rifles were upgraded with Picatinny rails, retractable stocks and new foregrips. This upgraded version was designated the AG-3F2. Various optical sights were also ordered beginning in October 2011, primarily Aimpoint CompM4s. The choice of Aimpoint is quite logical since it is a Swedish company.

FAR LEFT
Pictured taking part in a NATO exercise during August 1983, these Norwegian soldiers are armed with the AG-3 (Automatgevær 3, or 'assault rifle 3'), a variant of the G3 initially produced by Kongsberg Våpenfabrikk and then by Norsk Forsvarsteknologi in Norway. (SSgt Ernest Sealing/Wikimedia/Public Domain)

LEFT
Photographed during training in Germany in May 2008, this Norwegian soldier is armed with an AG-3F2 mounting an Aimpoint sight. (Spc Kalie Frantz/Wikimedia/Public Domain)

Although the 5.56×45mm assault rifle has proven popular in urban and jungle warfare, fighting in Afghanistan has shown once again the value of a rifle capable of engaging and eliminating an enemy at longer distances. Norway is a country in which engagement distances could quite conceivably be at longer ranges. As a result, it will be interesting to see, especially with heightened NATO awareness of a renewed Russian threat, if a decision is made to convert a substantial number of AG-3 rifles to AG-3F2 configuration. Iceland, which does not have an army as such, uses AG-3 rifles supplied by Norway; their primary use would be with the Icelandic Coast Guard and Crisis Response Unit.

The G3 also proved a popular choice among Baltic countries. As countries from the Baltic region have joined NATO, they have subsequently transitioned to 5.56×45mm rifles such as the G36. Estonia adopted the G3 upon leaving the Soviet sphere of influence, with rifles being acquired from Sweden, Norway and Germany. In addition to the Swedish AK4 and Norwegian AG-3F, Estonia has also fielded the G3A3ZF and G3A4. Estonia deployed troops to Afghanistan where the G3A3ZF was fielded as a DMR. Alongside the 7.62×51mm G3 variants, Estonia also uses 5.56×45mm variants of the Galil. Latvia's ground forces use the Swedish AK4, but it is being replaced by the G36. Latvia has supplied troops for various peacekeeping missions and for service in Afghanistan, so it is possible that their AK4s have been used in combat. Lithuania has also used the AK4, but the G36 replaced it. Lithuania has had a sustained commitment in Afghanistan, including by special forces, so its G36 rifles have been fired in anger.

South-East Europe

Among other NATO members who have used the G3 are Greece and Turkey. The Greek firm Elliniki Viomichania Oplon (EVO: Hellenic Arms Industry) manufactured the G3 under licence. Discussion boards featuring contributions from Greek veterans suggest that the G3 was

BELOW LEFT
In September 1991, a Greek National Guardsman armed with a G3A1 peers through a peephole in his sandbagged position, in the Greek-held area of Cyprus. Because of the tight quarters in the bunker he has the G3A1's stock collapsed. (David Rubinger/The LIFE Images Collection/Getty Images)

BELOW RIGHT
In January 2015, Greek soldiers fire a salute during the funeral ceremony for two Greek Air Force pilots who died during a NATO exercise. They use G3A3 rifles with black furniture, presumably manufactured under licence by EVO. (Pacific Press/LightRocket via Getty Images)

most appreciated for its simplicity. Some expressed the view that more modern assault rifles are over-engineered, which affects their battlefield reliability. Many also appreciate that the 7.62×51mm cartridge used in the G3 is well suited to combat in the Balkans and Turkey, where engagement ranges may be longer: 5.56×45mm rifles may not have the range needed for combat in those theatres. The view is also expressed, though, that the Turkish Army has considered replacing the G3 with the HK417, the 7.62×51mm version of the HK416. If so, this would indicate that the belief in the need for a harder-hitting, longer-ranged cartridge is felt within the Turkish military hierarchy as well.

Not all Greek veterans advocate as strongly for the G3 and the 7.62×51mm cartridge. Some found the G3 over-sized and clumsy. However, this view seems to arise particularly when considering urban combat. Some observers point out that within the Turkish armed forces, the regular infantry has used the G3, while special-operations forces use weapons chambered for the 5.56×45mm cartridge, such as the M4, though Turkish special-operations troops have also used the FN SCAR-H rifle, which chambers the 7.62×51mm cartridge.

An interesting aspect of the G3 rifles used by Turkish forces was noticeable in photographs taken during the attempted coup in Turkey in July 2016. Trigger guards of the rifles had been equipped with large protective shields, presumably for riot duty. It is not clear whether the intent was to prevent anyone attempting to snatch a soldier's rifle from pulling the trigger, or to make it more difficult for a soldier to discharge the rifle unintentionally.

In the Balkans, Croatian troops deployed during peacekeeping missions have used the G36, but the standard infantry weapons are the VHS and VHS2 bullpup assault rifles, chambered in 5.56×45mm and produced in Croatia by HS Produkt. The Georgian armed forces still use the AK-74 and AKS-74 as their standard rifle, but they do have 2,500 G3s provided by Turkey; these may be used as DMRs. The Macedonian armed forces rely primarily on various rifles produced by Zastava Arms of Serbia, but they do have some G3 rifles and also some US M4 carbines, the latter probably supplied to Macedonian troops serving in Afghanistan. Standard arms of the Serbian armed forces are domestically produced Zastava assault rifles, but Serbian special forces use the G36.

In August 2014, during joint training conducted at Izmir, Turkey, by troops from 21 countries, a Republic of Korea Armed Forces soldier fires a 5.56×45mm HK33E rifle produced under licence by MKEK. Note the polymer 30-round magazine. (Emin Menguarslan/Anadolu Agency/Getty Images)

G3 variants in British service

Another NATO member that has used the G3, albeit in limited numbers, is the United Kingdom. The HK53 has been used extensively by British special forces. Its compact size and firepower combined with the 5.56×45mm chambering made it especially popular on undercover assignments when ambush was a possibility. Full-sized G3s were used for special purposes.

The British Special Boat Service (SBS) used a scoped G3 rifle for helicopter-borne snipers supporting ship-boarding operations for many years. Whether this was the G3A3ZF with a Hensoldt 4-power scope or the G3SG/1 with a Zeiss 6-power scope is not clear. Normally, for this type of sniping a wider field of view is desirable, so the 4-power scope may have been chosen.

An interesting incident involving two SBS snipers and their G3 rifles occurred when they were being flown on a training mission to a firing range in the United Kingdom by HRH Prince Andrew, who was at the time a Royal Navy helicopter pilot (Falconer 1998: 330–31). Clad in black one-piece coveralls and armed with G3 rifles, the two snipers offered the Prince coffee from their flasks, but he declined and suggested they land for tea nearby at a 'friend's'. They landed at the Sandringham country estate in Norfolk where they were greeted by a number of security men. After the Prince explained that they were just stopping for tea, the SBS operators started to follow him, but the security men informed them that they would have to leave their rifles, to which they replied that they would not, having been trained never to do so. The Prince pointed out that few were better qualified to carry weapons into Sandringham than members of the Special Boat Service. The Queen greeted her son and the two SBS snipers at the door and, noticing their rifles, told the snipers to put their weapons in a nearby umbrella stand. The Queen served them

The author firing the HK53, a weapon that has proved to be very popular with British special-forces units because of its compact size and firepower. (Author)

tea, then escorted them to the door where they retrieved their G3s, boarded the helicopter, and set off to complete their training. The story is entertaining, but also highlights the fact that the Royal Family was quite secure in the competency with their weapons and loyalty of the men serving in the Special Boat Service.

Shorter versions of the HK33 (the HK53) and the G3 (the G3K) were especially popular with British undercover units in Northern Ireland, especially 14th Intelligence Company, which would evolve into today's Special Reconnaissance Regiment. Although the HK MP5K submachine gun was widely used by members of 14th Intelligence Company as it could be easily concealed and offered close-range firepower to break an ambush, often something heavier was needed to deal with members of the Provisional Irish Republican Army (PIRA) travelling in vehicles or armed with rifles. One instructor, noting that the unit normally eschewed weapons chambering the 5.56×45mm round as they were harder to conceal than 9mm weapons while lacking the stopping power offered by the 7.62×51mm cartridge, praised the HK53 as a reliable, accurate weapon that provided an excellent compromise between compactness and firepower. The same instructor rated the G3K highly as it offered devastating firepower on full-auto, but noted that PIRA members also carried the G3, their rifles having been obtained via Libya (Rennie 1996: 111–12). After a continued discussion of the use of lights and infrared filters on the various weapons, members of 14th Intelligence Company proceeded to shoot the weapons on the range. This unit contained female operators who were fully trained in weapons usage. One such operator, her small stature making it difficult for her to control the G3K, opted to choose the HK53 instead, as its recoil was negligible (Rennie 1996: 113).

Displaying a high degree of professionalism about their weapons, upon which they relied every time they went out onto the streets, each time members of 14th Intelligence Company drew their HK53 or G3K weapons they zeroed these weapons on the 'pipe range' (normally, a compact underground range that requires shooting through a pipe), after which they zeroed their MP5Ks and pistols in the 'killing room', the Close Quarters Battle (CQB) training range (Rennie 1996: 150). One member of 14th Intelligence Company noted the weapons he chose when kitting up before going on an operation. Alongside the two pistols he tucked into his clothing, he loaded his HK53 with a double magazine – the two clamped together using an HK component – and placed two spare magazines in a bag with a stun grenade and other kit (Rennie 1996: 164).

British troops also encountered the G3 in use in Northern Ireland. Formed in 1986, the Irish People's Liberation Organization (IPLO) was a paramilitary group known for carrying out assassinations. The IPLO experienced bitter internal struggles that resulted in the deaths of two well-known figures, Jimmy Brown and Sammy Ward, who were shot and killed in August and November 1992 respectively. During the bloodletting that followed these deaths, the G3 played a grim role; PIRA foot patrols tracked down IPLO members, some of whom were shot in the hands and legs with the G3s, the rifles deliberately chosen over pistols as they inflicted more severe wounds.

The Hensoldt 4-power scope widely used on the G3. (Author)

G3 SCOPES

The 4-power optical sight on a STANAG claw mount was widely used on the G3 rifle, allowing the weapon to function as a marksman's rifle – a DMR, in later terminology. Three optics companies produced scopes for the Bundeswehr: Schmidt & Bender, Karl Kaps and Hensoldt. By far the largest number of scopes were supplied by Hensoldt, which is actually the brand name for Zeiss's military optics.

Three versions of the Hensoldt scope were produced. They vary in type of reticle, presence or absence of a focus knob and presence or absence of click adjustments. The most common version is the second type, which has a reticle that can be illuminated and a focus knob on the right side. Windage and elevation turrets do not have internal click adjustments. This scope will normally be in a G3 STANAG claw mount.

All of the versions have a bullet-drop compensator for 7.62×51mm NATO ammunition, with the numbers '1' to '6' designating distances from 100m to 600m. The reticle is graded in mils (from mildot), with 1 mil equal to 1m at 1,000m. Thus, at 100m, 1 mil equals 10cm. At 100m, the field of view is 102m. With practice, a marksman could quickly estimate range by using the mil divisions on the cross bars as they relate to a 'known' width. For example, a typical Soviet BMD-1 infantry fighting vehicle is 2.53m wide. If, therefore, the BMD-1 when viewed fitted almost exactly between two posts on the cross bar that measure 10 mils between them, this would indicate a range of approximately 250m, requiring an elevation setting between 2 and 3.

A Romanian soldier fires a G3 mounting the Hensoldt 4-power scope using a claw mount. (AirSeaLand Photos)

In this 1995 photograph, German *Scharfschützen* ('sharpshooters') of Jägerbataillon 581 are shown with G3 rifles mounting at left, what appears to be the Hensoldt 4×24mm scope, and at right, a night-vision scope, which appears to be the Zeiss Orion 80/1 Fero Z51. (P/F/H/ullstein bild via Getty Images)

Adjustments for windage were normally based on a table using wind speed and range. For example, at 5m/sec it would be necessary to use four clicks at 400m to adjust for windage.

There is also a Schmidt & Bender 6-power scope on a G3 STANAG claw mount that is much less common.

These troops are pictured during a parade marking the anniversary of the founding of the Turkish Republic of Northern Cyprus; the soldier at left has a night-vision scope mounted, while the soldier at right has a standard optical sight and night-vision goggles on his head. (BIROL BEBEK/AFP/Getty Images)

THE G3 IN AFRICA AND THE MIDDLE EAST SINCE 1991

The G3 has equipped various Middle Eastern armed forces and seen combat in Syria and Libya. Bahrain has used an array of rifles including the G3, FN FAL, M16 and M4 carbine. Jordan's well-trained and -equipped army has an array of rifles from the United States, China and Germany, including the G3 and G36. US M16 rifles and M4 carbines and Chinese T65 rifles and T86 carbines seem to be used more than the HK rifles at the time of writing. Jordanian forces are widely deployed on peacekeeping and training missions, in which it is possible that their weapons will be used; and Jordanian combat troops are deployed to South Yemen on counter-insurgency duty. The Lebanese armed forces have the G3 in their armoury, but it is now used primarily for training; the US M16 rifle is the standard infantry weapon. Given the continuous conflicts in Lebanon, it is likely that shots were fired in anger from Lebanese G3s at some point. The G3 has also been used by Qatar, as have the Finnish Valmet M62 and M76, the FN FAL, the AK-47 and the US M16A1, CAR15A1 and M4. The large influx of US weapons more recently has superseded the G3 in most Qatari units. Qatari forces have also seen combat in Yemen.

The G3 is manufactured under licence in Saudi Arabia and remains the standard infantry rifle of Saudi forces; Saudi troops armed with the G3 saw action in Operation *Desert Storm*. Saudi Arabia has also supplied G3s to other Middle Eastern countries. However, Saudi Arabia is now manufacturing the G36, which will replace the G3 in many units. The Syrian Republican Guard uses the G3A3 and G3A4 as DMRs. G3s from Turkey and Saudi Arabia have also turned up in the hands of various opposition factions in the Syrian Civil War (2011–present), alongside limited numbers of G36 and HK416 rifles. The United Arab Emirates has used both FN FAL and G3 rifles, but these are now in reserve, having been replaced by the 5.56×45mm CAR816 assault rifle manufactured in Abu Dhabi by Caracal International.

A substantial number of African countries have adopted the G3 rifle. The possibility of longer-range engagement in Africa has made a battle rifle such as the G3 appealing, but the training level of many African armies has made the AK-47 more popular because of its ability to keep functioning with less maintenance. To some extent, use of the G3 may be attributable to the Portuguese influence in Africa. Angola, a former Portuguese colony, used the G3 along with the FAL, but in the post-colonial era the AK-47 became the standard infantry weapon of Angolan forces. For many years, the G3 was the standard rifle of the Kenya Defence Forces, though the US M4A1 rifle has been replacing it in some elements of the KDF. Many former French colonies, including the Central African Republic, Chad, Côte d'Ivoire, Djibouti, Gabon, Mauritania and Niger, adopted the G3. Most African countries, however, field a mixed armoury of weapons, often dependent on who has been willing to supply them with military aid. Djibouti, for example, has the AKM, FAMAS, FN FAL, Galil, M4, SG540, Steyr AUG and Chinese Type 56 in its armouries in addition to the G3.

The First Gulf War and after

During the First Gulf War in 1990–91, several members of the United Nations Coalition deployed troops armed with the FN FAL, including Australia and Canada, while the contingents fielded by Qatar and Saudi Arabia carried the G3; the forces of Bahrain, Morocco, Turkey and the United Arab Emirates used both rifles during the conflict. As actual combat was brief and mostly involved US, British and French forces, it is unlikely that the G3 saw much combat.

For the purposes of this study, the important point is that the G3 has become so widely distributed that it turns up in most areas where there is conflict. According to some reports, G3 and G36 rifles in the hands of Islamic State of Iraq and Syria (ISIS) personnel are from stocks of weapons

BELOW LEFT
Saudi troops training in Saudi Arabia prior to Operation *Desert Storm*; the soldier in the foreground is armed with a G3A4, presumably produced in Saudi Arabia under licence. The design of the buttplate makes the G3A4's stock uncomfortable in recoil and makes the rifle hard to control during full-auto fire. (Tom Stoddart/Getty Images)

BELOW RIGHT
Iraq, November 2002: this Kurdish fighter on the front line against the Sunni Muslim Ansar al-Islam insurgency group is armed with a G3 rifle. During and after the 2003 invasion of Iraq, US and allied troops recovered surprisingly small numbers of unlicensed Iranian G3 copies, with only two sniping variants recorded in US intelligence assessments (Schroeder & King 2012: 322). This was not the case in Somalia during 2010–11, however, with 1,646 G3s reported captured (Schroeder & King 2012: 338). This is probably attributable to the fact that the G3 has been the issue rifle for the Somali armed forces for many years. (Scott Peterson/Getty Images)

delivered to the Kurdish Peshmerga since 2014. Weapons with 'HK' in the serial number and marked 'Bw' for Bundeswehr were reportedly for sale in arms markets outside Erbil, the capital of Kurdistan. Some claim that these weapons came from the 12,000 G3 rifles, 8,000 G36 rifles and 8,000 P1 pistols delivered to the Peshmerga by the Bundeswehr, with many of the guns for sale coming from Peshmerga fighters who had deserted and left the combat zone.

Since the invasion of Afghanistan in 2001, the G3 has been issued to Afghan military forces. Here, Afghan soldiers take part in military training at a Turkish commando training centre near Isparta in December 2009. They appear to be armed with MKEK-produced G3A7s. (ADEM ALTAN/AFP/Getty Images)

The G3 in Afghanistan

For the most part, German soldiers deployed to Afghanistan since 2001 have been armed with G36 rifles rather than G3s, though some G3s have been used as DMRs. Based on reports, the number of G3 rifles still available for use by the Bundeswehr has been reduced sharply, so it is likely that only a limited number remain in use. In the period 2001–07, more than 550,000 G3 rifles were destroyed as the number of Bundeswehr personnel decreased and new weapons were introduced (Beeck 2014).

OPPOSITE
In Afghanistan during 2011 a German designated marksman/sharpshooter assigned to the International Security Assistance Force (ISAF) is armed with the G3SG/1. These rifles were selected for their accuracy and modified with a heavy, dual-stage buffer. An adjustable set-trigger pack was added, the handguard was lengthened to take a bipod and the buttstock was given an adjustable cheek piece. The scope is the Zeiss Diavari-DA 1.5–6×35mm. (DVIDSHUB/Wikimedia/Public Domain)

The G3 in Bundeswehr service in Afghanistan (overleaf)

German troops in Afghanistan engage after being ambushed by the Taliban. The German troops have taken cover behind their KMW vehicle. Except for the designated marksman/sharpshooter with G3A3ZF in the foreground, the Germans are armed with the G36 rifle with the dual optical sight. A dead Taliban sniper lies in the foreground with his SVD rifle nearby.

IMPACT
A Cold War icon

DESIGN INFLUENCE

The modular design of the G3 allows it quickly to be altered to variants, such as the G3A4 paratroop model with collapsible stock. In addition to the stock and forearm, the trigger pack can be swapped among various weapons. HK has continued the modular trend in its subsequent rifle designs; the FN SCAR also offers substantial modularity, as do the Beretta ARX series and Colt's CM901, among others.

In the 1960s and after, HK continued development of other weapons based on the G3. As well as engendering the HK33, the 5.56×45mm version of the rifle, the G3's basic design would influence the HK21 general-purpose machine gun and the iconic HK MP5 submachine gun.

The HK21

Developed in 1961, the HK21 general-purpose machine gun has nearly 50 per cent parts interchangeability with the G3, and uses a modified version of the G3's receiver. Chambered in 7.62×51mm NATO, the weapon can be readily converted to the 7.62×39mm and 5.56×45mm chamberings favoured by some HK customers by swapping out the barrel, bolt and feed-plate unit. It can be either belt fed (from the left-hand side)

A right-side view of the HK21A1. Offering a rate of fire of 900rd/min over ranges up to 1,200m, the HK21A1 weighs 8.30kg and is 1,030mm long with a 450mm barrel. In its HK21A1 configuration, the HK21 took part in the US trials for a new Squad Automatic Weapon (SAW), but in 1982 the FN Minimi was adopted as the M249. (Armémuseum (The Swedish Army Museum)/Wikimedia/Public Domain)

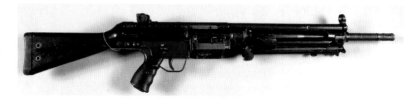

or magazine fed via an adaptor that permits use of the G3's 20-round box magazine or a 50-round drum magazine.

During the 1970s the HK21 was updated to feature a carrying handle and a hooked buttstock; it also incorporated polygonal rifling. The weapon was subsequently offered in two principal variants: the HK21A1 general-purpose machine gun and the HK11A1 automatic rifle. The 1980s saw further modernizations, with the range broadened to include the HK11E (7.62×51mm) and HK13E (5.56×45mm) automatic rifles and the HK21E (7.62×51mm) and HK23E (5.56×45mm) general-purpose machine guns. The versions of the weapons used by the Bundeswehr and Bundespolizei are designated the G8 and G8A1.

The MP5

An extremely popular descendant of the G3 is the HK MP5, the world's most widely used submachine gun. As with the G3 and other rifle-calibre HK weapons, the MP5 uses the roller-delayed blowback locking system. Unlike many SMGs, however, the MP5 fires from a closed bolt. The earliest versions of what would become the MP5 in 9×19mm calibre were introduced in 1964 as the HK9. By 1965, the designation had been changed to HK54 to fit the HK coding system, with '5' indicating a machine pistol and '4' indicating 9×19mm chambering. In 1966, the HK54 was adopted by the West German Bundespolizei (Federal Police), BGS and military special forces. After military adoption the weapon was designated the MP5. It was its use by GSG-9, the BGS counter-terrorist unit, that brought the MP5 to the attention of other military and police special forces assigned the counter-terrorist role, including the United Kingdom's Special Air Service. The MP5 is still widely used by military and law-enforcement special units today in myriad variations.

The G41

In October 1980, NATO members adopted the 5.56×45mm cartridge as a smaller calibre to eventually replace the 7.62×51mm NATO round. Instead of the US 55-grain (3.56g) M193 loading, the 62-grain (4.02g) SS109 (M855) round was chosen as the NATO standard. HK realized that to compete with the M16 and FN FNC assault rifles, the firm's designers would need to build on the legacy of the HK33. The result, introduced in 1981, was the G41. Features included: a longer barrel and shorter receiver than those of the HK33; a positive bolt-closing device; an M16-type ejection-port cover; an M16-type bolt hold-open device; and a carrying handle that rested on the left side of the receiver when not in use. The G41 was also designed so that it could take the NATO STANAG (Standardization Agreement) M16-type magazines, the STANAG scope base and a standard M16 (NATO) bipod. Its selector switch incorporated a three-round-burst mode. A G41K shorter version with retractable buttstock was also available. The G41 was tested by some NATO members, but was not adopted by any of them – probably because of the ubiquity of the M16 (Johnston & Nelson 2010: 441).

THE G3'S IMPACT ON THE ARMS TRADE

An important influence of the G3 is its part in developing the arms production capacity in many countries. A look at the number of countries that produced the G3 or HK33 under licence or without licence includes Burma/Myanmar, France, Greece, Iran, Norway, Pakistan, Portugal, Saudi Arabia, Spain, Sudan, Sweden, Turkey and the United Kingdom (Jones 2007: 173). The willingness of HK to license production was a substantial factor in many countries' adoption of the G3 rather than the FN FAL. Norway is a good example of an early adopter of the G3, despite the fact that the FAL rifle performed equally as well in Norwegian trials. Norway's primary reasons for adoption of the G3 were the lower unit cost, the ease of manufacture and HK's willingness to license production in Norway (Zhou 2016: 42).

In France, Manufacture d'armes de Saint-Étienne (MAS) produced the G3 for export to Lebanon, Haiti and Senegal, among others (Stevens 2006: 404–05). Stevens offers an additional insight into the French involvement in the supply of G3s and other HK products (Stevens 2006: 403). During

the Cold War, the West Berlin Police were not allowed to import weapons from West Germany. As a result, MAS assembled components made by HK into completed G3 rifles and MP5 submachine guns and marked them 'Made in France', thus allowing them to be shipped to West Berlin. The agreement with MAS would have become even more important had the HK33F, which performed very well in the 1974 competition for a new French military rifle, been selected. Though the HK33F proved superior to the other rifles in the tests, political considerations resulted in the French adoption of the 5.56×45mm FAMAS assault rifle.

From 1972, G3s were also assembled at Royal Small Arms Factory (RSAF) Enfield. These weapons were marketed in areas of traditional British influence, such as English-speaking Africa and the Middle Eastern Trucial States (Stevens 2006: 406). Eventually, a substantial number of parts for the G3 were produced at RSAF Enfield. Barrels were produced there and some were imported from Sweden. In 1988, production of HK weapons was moved to Royal Ordnance Factory (ROF) Nottingham. The relationship with HK became more complex when in 1991 Royal Ordnance (British Aerospace) purchased Heckler & Koch. The most noteworthy product produced at ROF Nottingham after the purchase was probably the HK33 rifle, with some 40,000 being produced for South American countries prior to this site being closed in 2001 (Stevens 2006: 411).

ABOVE LEFT
A Latvian soldier with the Swedish-produced AK4 version of the G3. (Tech Sgt Dawn M. Price/Wikimedia/Public Domain)

ABOVE RIGHT
Pictured in Iraq during March 2006, this Latvian soldier is armed with a G3 rifle: normally the Latvians used Swedish AK4 variants. (AirSeaLand Photos)

Two views of the G3's diopter rear sight set on the battle sight 'V' (**1**) and the 400m 'peep' setting (**2**), plus a view of the G3's hooded front post sight (**3**); note also the front attachment point for the sling. Among those who have positive views of the G3, the rotary diopter sight is viewed as an aid to accuracy. The G3 also allows relatively easy mounting of an optical sight using the HK claw mount. (Author)

THE FN FAL VERSUS THE G3

By far the most popular battle rifles in use during the Cold War and, to some extent, today, are the G3 and the FN FAL. Determining exactly how many of each have been built is difficult, as so many were built under licence or as unlicensed copies, but there were many millions produced. Among NATO members, the choice of G3 or FN FAL was relatively evenly split. The G3 has been used by the armed forces of Denmark (Gv/M66), Norway (AG-3), and Spain (CETME), while the FN FAL has been adopted by the armed forces of Belgium, Luxembourg and the Netherlands; some NATO countries – (West) Germany, Greece, Portugal, Turkey and the United Kingdom – have issued both weapons. Both rifles were equally popular in other parts of the world, often both turning up in trouble-spots. To some extent, both have remained relevant by taking on the DMR role, as with the US M14, but the G3 seems to have carried out this mission more often, at least partially due to the large number of Hensoldt 4-power scopes and claw mounts produced.

As the size and weight of the G3 became an issue once other NATO armies adopted lighter rifles in 5.56×45mm calibre, it would be useful to give the specifications for the G3 as delivered to the Bundeswehr and other armed forces. The G3A3 (and the G3A4 with stock extended) measure 1,026mm overall; with stock collapsed, the G3A4 is 841mm long. Barrel length is 450mm. The G3A3 weighs 4.10kg, while the G3A4 weighs 4.54kg. By comparison, the FN FAL with fixed stock is 1,092mm overall and weighs 4.30kg; barrel length is 533mm.

One commentator (Zhou 2016) points out some of the pros and cons of the G3 versus the FAL. Many of the conclusions are drawn from an Aberdeen Proving Ground evaluation of the G3; information from West German testing of the G3 versus the FAL was also incorporated.

One important point raised by evaluators was the 'manufacturing advantages' offered by the G3. Based on the Bundeswehr's experience, the G3 was less sensitive to dirt than the FAL (Zhou 2016: 42). The Aberdeen Proving Ground evaluation also found that the G3 could function more effectively in adverse conditions (Carlson & Golm 1969: 42–43). An interesting point made in the Aberdeen Proving Ground evaluation was that the G3, even though it had a stamped receiver, could be rebuilt up to eight times, thus greatly increasing service life. However, it was also found that the G3 extractor spring could be bent, causing failures to extract. (Zhou 2016: 43). The FAL was rated positively for ergonomics.

A factor in favour of the FAL was its adjustable gas system that allowed field adjustments to enable the use of varying lots of ammunition. The G3 required different angles on its locking pieces to adjust for differences in ammunition pressure, thus making the rifle more sensitive, with adjustments difficult in the field. Some types of NATO ammunition would have required the G3's locking pieces to be changed (Zhou 2016: 43). Zhou concluded that if the G3 had been designed to function reliably with all NATO ammunition without the need to change locking pieces, its reliability and low cost would have made it the pre-eminent battle rifle of the Cold War period (Zhou 2016: 45).

The present author has fired thousands of rounds from both the G3/HK91 and FN FAL and can offer some conclusions from those experiences. Both are reliable rifles; the G3 does have some advantages as it lacks a gas system, which can become fouled. The lack of a gas system also means that the G3 is not as likely to malfunction with a lighter load; and, with a heavy load, the roller-locking system will remain locked more securely until pressure lessens. The FAL can also deal with ammunition of varying power by adjusting its gas valve. A downside of the G3's roller-

This photograph of West German recruits cleaning weapons, *c.*1984, offers a good view of the G3 stock removed and the bolt dropped out of the receiver for cleaning. The sling has also been removed and rolled up. (Ulrich Baumgarten via Getty Images)

German recruits disassembling their G3 rifles, *c.*1996. It is interesting that the older wooden-stocked G3 seems to have continued in use for training purposes. The G3's bolt does not remain open after the last round in the magazine is fired. Many consider this a disadvantage, as the shooter may not realize the magazine is empty before hearing the click of the action with an empty chamber. Some users of the G3 trained their troops to load tracer ammunition as the last two or three rounds in a magazine, so as to alert them that they were nearly empty. (Melde Bildagentur/ ullstein bild via Getty Images)

West German troops deploying from a Schützenpanzer Lang HS.30 infantry fighting vehicle, c.1972. The soldier on the ground grasps a G3 by the handguard, demonstrating how the length of the rifle made it unwieldy in vehicles, while the soldier about to jump from the vehicle carries an MG3. In standard infantry configuration, the G3 is shorter and lighter than the standard FN FAL or US M14, a positive feature in an era when the use of armoured personnel carriers and helicopters was revolutionizing warfare. Although the M14 did not have a folding-stock version designed for airborne troops, the G3, like the FN FAL, did have a paratroop version, the G3A4. Note, too, that the full-sized G3 is about the same overall length as the M16 assault rifle; the G3A4 with stock collapsed is shorter. (ullstein bild/ullstein bild via Getty Images)

locking system versus the FN FAL's gas operating system is that recoil always seems to be magnified with the G3, especially on full-auto fire.

Despite the G3 being shorter and lighter than the FAL, I have normally found that the Belgian rifle seems livelier in the hands, perhaps because of its better balance. I can normally shoot the FAL offhand better than the G3, though the difference in group size will normally be 3cm or less. The G3's rotary diopter rear sight gives it an advantage for accurate shooting over the FAL's aperture rear sight, especially when using a bipod or from a rest. The FAL's rear sight also seems more fragile, though I have not read accounts of it being broken in combat. Both rifles have a protective shield or protective 'ears' for the front sight.

The fixed stocks and pistol grips for both rifles are about equally comfortable in use; however, the FAL Para model's stock is distinctly better than the G3A4 stock. The rather small buttplate of the G3's collapsible stock concentrates recoil and makes it uncomfortable to shoot even on semi-auto and harder to control the rifle on full-auto. The FAL Para's folding stock is much more comfortable for shooting, though the cheek rests on the metal tube, which can be uncomfortable in cold weather. I like the pistol grip on the G3 a little more than that of the FAL. Not only do I find the G3's pistol grip more comfortable, but I also find that I can reach the selector switch with my thumb more readily.

G3 OPERATING SEQUENCE

Although the G3 operating sequence is straightforward, there are a couple of techniques that must be learned in order to bring the weapon into action quickly. Although pulling back of the cocking handle (**1**) may be carried out after loading a magazine into the magazine well, the difficulty of pulling the bolt handle all the way to the rear to ensure that a round is fully chambered – thus preventing a failure to feed during loading – often makes another technique more desirable. The cocking handle may be pulled back and locked into the cut-out in the receiver prior to loading the magazine. This same action may be carried out to allow checking of the chamber or otherwise dealing with a failure to feed should one occur.

With the bolt locked to the rear, the magazine may be rocked into position and locked in place (**2**). The system for locking the G3 magazine in place is well designed to present the cartridges for reliable feeding. Note that many armies that used the G3 reversed the steps just described. To allow the weapon to be carried safely, the magazine was loaded with the bolt forward, thus allowing the rifle to be carried with an empty chamber. If action were anticipated, the bolt could be

pulled back and released to load a round, or it could be locked into the cut-out.

Assuming the bolt has been locked into the cut-out in the receiver, it may then be slapped free (**3**) to run forward with maximum force to ensure reliable chambering of a cartridge. The selector will normally have been in the 'S' (safe) position. Once a round is chambered and the rifle is ready for action, the selector will remain in the 'S' (safe) position. When preparing to fire the rifle, it may be shifted to the 'E' (single shot/semi-automatic) setting or the 'F' (fully automatic) position (**4**). When a target is identified, the G3 will be placed against the shoulder, the target acquired, the selector moved off 'S' (safe) if this has not already been done, and the trigger pulled to engage the target (**5**).

Unlike some other battle or assault rifles, the bolt of the G3 does not remain open after the last round in the magazine is fired. Once the magazine is empty, the bolt may be locked to the rear or left in the forward position and the empty magazine removed by pressing the release flipper with the thumb and rocking the magazine out of the magazine well with the hand (**6**). The loading drill to continue engaging may then begin again.

The HK-manufactured .22-calibre G3 conversion unit was produced to enable less expensive training and/or training on indoor ranges not designed for the use of full-power rifle loads. Those produced by HK are of high quality and have a reputation for functioning well. Each kit included a wooden case for storage and transport, a bolt group, a barrel insert tube, two magazines and a cleaning kit. Some kits also included a manual. Prior to West Germany's adoption of the G3, conversion units were also produced for the FN FAL (G1). Initially, these were manufactured by ERMA Werke; reportedly, these did not function reliably, however. HK then received a contract to produce G1 conversion units that functioned reliably. When the G3 was adopted, HK was also given the contract to produce sub-calibre training units. It seems likely that all of the G3 units were produced by HK. (Author)

Both the G3 and FAL have cocking handles that are hinged and which fold when not in use – a good feature for keeping them out of the way. Both are also on the left side of the rifle, allowing a right-handed shooter to keep the shooting hand on the pistol grip while operating the cocking handle. I have found that the FAL's cocking handle seems easier to pull fully to the rear to chamber a round than that of the G3. In fact, if there is no need for a hurried loading operation, with the G3 I usually pull the cocking handle into the slot on the cocking tube and then slap it to bring the bolt forward and load a round. Both rifles have the magazine release located behind the magazine well to allow operation by the thumb of either hand; the best method is to operate the release with the thumb while pulling the empty magazine free. I find the G3's paddle release to be slightly quicker. I like the FAL's bolt release and find it easy to operate with the thumb after pushing a new magazine home. As the G3 lacks a hold-open device, it is necessary to pull back the cocking handle to load a fresh round after replacing an empty magazine. This lack of a hold-open can be a negative factor in combat, as the user will not know the rifle is empty until it goes, 'Click!'

As the two most widely used 7.62×51mm NATO rifles of the Cold War, the FAL and the G3 should have been in the hands of soldiers who had trained with them and knew their idiosyncrasies. The users of these rifles should have been trained well enough to adapt to the weapons. I have fired both of these rifles enough to understand their idiosyncrasies and appreciate their advantages. I'll admit to a preference for the FAL, but I would still consider myself well-armed with a G3.

THE G3 AND HK33 IN CIVILIAN AND LAW-ENFORCEMENT USE

The semi-automatic G3 and HK33

HK proved to be more aware than many other makers of military rifles of the potential civilian and law-enforcement markets for semi-automatic versions of the G3 and later the HK33. To understand the designations for these versions it is important to understand the numerical coding system used by HK. The first digit indicates the type of weapon and the second digit the calibre. The number '9' indicates a semi-automatic rifle according to the US Bureau of Alcohol, Tobacco, Firearms and Explosives (ATF) rules, while the number '1' indicates 7.62×51mm calibre; hence, the semi-automatic version of the G3 was designated the HK91. The number '3' indicates 5.56×45mm calibre; hence, the semi-automatic version of the HK33 was designated the HK93.

HK91 semi-automatic versions of the G3 were normally produced with the button magazine release shown here rather than the paddle one used on the G3. (Author)

Although the primary market for the semi-automatic version of the G3 was the United States, there would have also been a market in some other countries. The primary change was to render the sporting version incapable of full-automatic fire. A slight alteration in the dimensions of the HK91's trigger housing precluded the use of a select-fire G3 trigger housing. The HK91 trigger housing only offers two selector settings: a white '0' for safe and a red '1' for single shot (semi-automatic). Another change was in the magazine release, from the flipper style of the G3 to a push-button type on the HK91. Both an HK91A2 version with fixed stock and HK91A3 with collapsible stock were imported into the United States. Actually, under the designation Model 41, the HK91A2 was imported into the United States by Golden State Arms in 1963, making it the first of the foreign semi-automatic 'assault rifles' available to US shooters.

Owing to a change in US law, as of 1989 military-lookalike rifles such as the HK91 were banned. HK had approximately 1,000 HK91 rifles awaiting import into the United States when the import ban went into effect. In response, to make the rifles less 'military' HK changed the stock from one with a pistol grip to one with a thumbhole stock, and the flash hider was eliminated. Each rifle was supplied with a five-round magazine, though 20-round G3 magazines would still work. This modified version was known as the Model 911, though the designation had nothing to do with the 11 September 2001 attacks on New York and the Pentagon.

One of the earliest semi-automatic versions of the G3 imported into the United States by Golden State Arms. These are highly prized and have been known to sell to HK collectors for US$12,000–$15,000. (Courtesy of Rock Island Auction Services)

A top view of the HK93A2 with the Beta C magazine in place. This magazine may also be used in the HK33. It is designed to alternate feed from each of the dual drums to keep the magazine from overbalancing to one side. The magazine allows the user to fire from the prone position and is well balanced enough for ease of carrying the rifle. There is also a 100-round Beta C magazine available for the G3/HK91, but it adds substantial weight to the already heavy rifle. (Author)

AN HK93A2 shown at top and an HK91A3 with Hensoldt 4-power scope in claw mount shown at bottom for size comparison. The HK91A3's two-position selector switch for safe and single shot (semi-automatic) is clearly visible; the HK93A2 has the same style of selector switch. (Author)

To continue legal importation of a version of the HK91, HK designed the SR9, which retained the thumbhole stock and the barrel without a flash hider. Rifling was also changed on these rifles to polygonal and a new buffer system was incorporated. An SR9 (T) (T for 'target') version was made with the stock, precision trigger group and adjustable pistol grip from the PSG-1 precision rifle. Reportedly, 48,817 HK91 rifles were imported into the United States before the imposition of the 1989 ban. This figure includes both A2 and A3 models, the latter of which have always brought a premium. These rifles are still highly sought after by shooters and collectors in the United States. Some G3-type semi-automatic rifles were also imported from elsewhere, though not in large quantities. For example, a limited number of rifles produced by EVO in Greece were imported by Springfield Armory as the SAR-8.

The semi-automatic version of the HK33, the HK93, was also rendered incapable of fully automatic fire and employed the push-button magazine release. Far fewer HK93 rifles were imported into the United States prior to the 1989 ban, and when the ban went into effect HK did not make a 'de-militarized' version for import.

A semi-automatic version of the CETME rifle was also produced for the US Mars Equipment Corporation and tested in 1964 by the Alcohol and Tobacco Tax Division (ATTD), the predecessor to the ATF, which found that it qualified as a semi-automatic rifle. As part of precluding conversion of the CETME to full-auto, the selector switch was moved from the right to the left side of the receiver. In fact, the ATTD ruled that the HK91 and the Colt AR15 semi-automatic rifles being sold in the United States could be more readily converted to full-auto than the CETME (Stevens 2006: 445). A total of 1,258 CETME 'Sport' versions were imported into the United States (Stevens 2006: 449).

Parts-kit G3 and CETME rifles in the United States

Although the United States is normally the largest market for civilian sales of military-style sporting rifles, G3 and CETME battle rifles could not be imported into that country. Other than for very limited sales to military or law-enforcement agencies, the select-fire military version would have been banned in any case, but for many years semi-automatic versions of foreign-built 'assault rifles' have been banned as well.

This does not mean, however, that the large number of surplus G3s and CETMEs have not had an influence on the US sporting-rifle market. Parts kits that do not include the receiver and, as of 2005, the barrel are legally importable. These kits can then be assembled using a US-made receiver and, unless the kit was imported before 2005, a US-made barrel. To complicate matters for the fabricator of G3s assembled from parts kits in the United States, the ATF has a list of 20 key component parts, of which no more than ten may have been manufactured outside the United States. Nevertheless, a substantial number of these 'parts kit' G3s have been assembled over the last decade.

One of the largest producers and sellers of these guns is Century International Arms (CIA), which has produced semi-automatic versions of the G3 and CETME using parts kits. The other primary manufacturer/assembler of the G3 using parts is PTR Industries, which produces the PTR-91 FR. Receivers for PTR are made on the original equipment used in Portugal to produce the G3 there. This tooling, originally supplied by HK, was purchased by JLD Enterprises, the forerunner of PTR Industries, from Fábrica de Braço de Prata in Portugal. PTR Industries receivers are used by other companies that assemble parts-kit G3s. The polymer trigger group produced by PTR Industries is also used in other kit-guns, including, to the best of this author's knowledge, those produced by Century International Arms. Actually, although PTR Industries originally imported many surplus parts, it currently manufactures new parts in the United States.

One advantage of the PTR-91 FR is the use of the flipper magazine release instead of the button type of the HK91. The C308 uses the button magazine release. Due to the oddities of California law relating to 'assault rifles', the magazine release on a PTR-91 for sale in the state must consist of what is known as a 'bullet button', a device that requires a tool to remove the magazine rather than the finger or thumb. Although the PTR-91 F is the basic G3 clone, PTR Industries also manufactures variants including sniper and carbine versions.

Century International Arms' current version of the G3, the C308, incorporates a Picatinny rail for easy mounting of optical sights and a CIA-sourced muzzle brake. The rear sight is of the flip-up leaf type used on the CETME rifle. Reportedly, CIA purchased all remaining CETME surplus. According to Stevens, the castings for CIA receivers are produced by a highly skilled aerospace manufacturer (Stevens 2006: 469). The C308 has proven popular with US shooters and current production versions are considered to be of good quality. (Century International Arms)

REPLACING THE G3

During the Cold War, there were sound reasons for NATO forces to field a battle rifle firing the 7.62×51mm NATO round. If the Warsaw Pact countries attacked across the North German Plain the 7.62×51mm round would offer longer range and better penetration than the 7.62×39mm round fired by the AK-47. On the other hand, 7.62×51mm battle rifles proved very difficult to control on full-auto fire, thus negating much of their tactical *raison d'étre*. The United States, the United Kingdom and other NATO members experimented with lighter assault-rifle cartridges. During the 1960s, US involvement in the jungle counter-insurgency war in Vietnam hastened the development and adoption of the 5.56×45mm round and the M16 assault rifle and by May 1967, the M16 had officially replaced the M14 as the US service rifle, though US troops assigned to NATO in Europe would continue to use the M14 for a time. By the time US forces finally left Vietnam in 1975, the M16 and the 5.56×45mm cartridge had seen substantial combat, allowing them to be substantially improved. By comparison, despite being widely issued, the 7.62×51mm round and the various battle rifles firing it had seen relatively little sustained combat.

The United States' pre-eminent position in NATO compelled other members to consider the 5.56×45mm round and in 1980, it was approved as a second NATO standard alongside the 7.62×51mm NATO round. NATO members began to consider adoption of rifles chambered for the 5.56×51mm round, with the British and French moving towards bullpup designs in the SA80/L85 and the FAMAS respectively. FN had developed the FNC assault rifle during the later 1970s; Italy developed the AR70, while Spain began developing the CETME Model L in 1981. Although HK had offered the HK33 in 5.56×45mm calibre for export as a competitor to the M16 since 1968, the West German firm foresaw West Germany moving towards an even more modern design: the G11.

A wooden mock-up of the G11. Visible features include the high mounted optical sight to allow a proper cheek weld with the bullpup stock, the four-position selector switch and the top-mounted magazine. Three magazines could be fitted atop the G11, the one feeding the rifle plus two spares. The G11 was tested as part of the US Advanced Combat Rifle (ACR) Program, which began in 1986 to find a replacement for the M16. The K2 version of the G11 that participated in the ACR trials employed an innovative 45-round magazine located atop the rifle, but the trials ended in 1990 without adoption of any of the weapons tested. Ultimately, no country other than West Germany had shown significant interest in the rifle. (© Royal Armouries PR.13162)

The G11

Although the Bundeswehr had previously considered adopting a 5.56×45mm rifle, instead, it was expected that the HK G11, a bullpup assault rifle firing caseless 4.73×33mm ammunition, would be adopted. Development of the G11 was completed *c.*1990, just as the Cold War came to a close and the two Germanies moved towards reunification;

1,000 G11 rifles were produced and underwent field trials with the Bundeswehr, but ultimately, the G11 was not adopted. Among the reasons was excessive heat build-up, as the 4.73×33mm round had no metal case to absorb heat from the chamber.

The G36

Although the HK33 had been designed in an attempt to offer a 5.56×45mm rifle to conform to NATO adoption of this calibre, there was a renewed impetus to design a new, less expensive 5.56×45mm rifle after the purchase of HK by Royal Ordnance in March 1991. During development, the new rifle was initially called Project50, then HK50, then eventually the HK36. This rifle never went into full production, however. Instead, some innovations from the HK50/HK36 project were incorporated into the Gewehr 36 (G36) that would eventually emerge (Johnston & Nelson 2010: 466–67). Many of the countries that had previously used the G3 later adopted the G36; it was adopted by the Bundeswehr in 1997.

Notably, the G36 did not use the roller-delayed blowback system of the G3. Instead, a lugged, rotating bolt similar to that used in the M16 rifle was incorporated, along with a short-stroke gas piston. Also, instead of metal stampings, the G36 uses carbon-fibre reinforced polymer for most parts. The only steel part in the upper receiver is a bar that unlocks and guides the bolt cam. The bolt carrier is of machined steel. The rotating bolt removes the need for the G3's fluted chamber, so cases ejected from the G36 do not show the distinctive striations found on fired G3 or HK33 brass cases (Johnston & Nelson 2010: 467–69). The G36 has a twist of 1-in-7, which optimizes it for use of the NATO-standard SS108/M855 cartridge.

Variants of the G36 include: the MG36, a SAW version with heavier barrel; the G36K carbine, with a 318mm barrel; and the G36C, with a 229mm barrel. All versions have a side-folding stock. The selector for the G36 variants is marked with the international symbols used on the HK MP5 and other weapons. These consist of coloured bullets – white for safe, one red for semi-auto, two red for two-round burst, three red for three-round burst and, normally, five red for full-auto.

The G36 rifle in 5.56×45mm NATO. Among the noteworthy features of the G36 are an ambidextrous selector, 30-round magazine, side-folding stock, and a ZF optical sight which incorporates a 3-power sight designed for zeroing at 200m and has bullet-drop calibration for 400m, 600m and 800m; atop the ZF is a non-magnified reflex sight for close-quarter battle. One important feature of the G3 that is retained in the G36 is modularity. By pushing out an assembly pin, various parts may be readily switched. Included are the trigger group and the magazine well, thus allowing STANAG magazines or proprietary HK G36 magazines to be used. The polymer HK magazines are designed so that they may be fastened together to allow a faster magazine change. The detachable carrying handle of the G36 houses the standard 1.5-power optical sight. A Hensoldt Passive Night Vision module was designed for use with this sight. Many military users, including the Bundeswehr, have ordered the G36 with a dual sight that also incorporates a 3.5-power optical sight containing a battery-operated red dot with stadia lines to 800m (Johnston & Nelson 2010: 469). (© Royal Armouries PR.13207)

THE G36 IN AFGHANISTAN

Reports suggest that German soldiers stationed in Afghanistan were not fully satisfied with their G36 rifles; one issue stemmed from the differences between the version of the rifle issued to German troops and the version sold for export to other armed forces. The German-issue version has a built-in reflex sight, while the export version has iron sights. There are reports that some German soldiers have broken off the reflex site and unsuccessfully tried to restore the iron sights. I have fired the Bundeswehr version of the G36 and find its dual sight system quite usable. For distance, the magnified 3-power sight with reticle graduated for various distances works well, as does the reflex sight mounted atop the telescopic sight. Why the German soldiers would want to remove the optical sights to use iron sights is unclear, unless this is based on the assumption that both optical sights would be damaged and unusable.

Another fault that led to malfunctions became apparent during combat use in Afghanistan. The plastic parts in the G36 trigger group were subject to excessive wear from the grit that got into the action during operations in harsh environments. There were also complaints that the G36 proved fragile in combat and was inaccurate. Some accounts state that the G36 became inaccurate after firing only five magazines in sustained fire. In 2009, reports appeared that the G36 was overheating in combat. These reports were validated on Good Friday, 2 April 2010, when German troops saw their most intense combat since World War II. During a ten-hour firefight against the Taliban in the Char Darrah district, three German paratroopers were killed during an engagement in which the unit fired 28,000 rounds. Subsequent investigations showed that no Taliban personnel were critically injured during the engagement. More tellingly, helmet-camera footage combined with eyewitness accounts demonstrated that the G36s did indeed overheat, requiring troops to let the weapons cool off before they could re-engage the enemy.

It seems to this author that the issues of overheating and inaccuracy are far more important than those related to the sights unless the latter have proven especially fragile in combat. The German Army was experiencing its most intense combat since World War II in this firefight with the Taliban, though compared to the combat experiences of US, British, French and other troops since World War II it was relatively minor. Combat tests weapon design under real and harsh conditions. Those weapons that have seen extensive combat will normally have had problems addressed when encountered. The US M4A1 has now been used in combat in various places over many years and has been improved based on the battlefield experience. The G36, though a lightweight design appreciated by troops who have to carry it, may not be appreciated when in combat. Likewise, its vaunted ergonomics are not as important as its ability to keep operating when facing the enemy. The G3, on the other hand, though heavy, engendered confidence in the troops. (It should be noted that many US troops in Afghanistan also found the M4A1 carbine lacking for long-range engagement, thus resulting in a substantial number of M14 rifles being brought out of storage for use as DMRs.)

Reportedly, the German armed forces are now being equipped with an 'improved' version of the G36 that includes a modular reflex sight instead of the integrated one. The rifle's unreliability continues to be an issue, however, to the extent that in the summer of 2014, the Bundeswehr halted purchases of the G36 (Rimmele 2014). It has been reported that the German Army would like to replace the G36 with the HK416 version of the Colt M4. As of 2018, the HK433, a modular rifle/carbine with some similarities to the US SCAR is considered a candidate to replace the G36.

US Army soldier Spc Amanda Luna, 1st Aviation Regiment, fires a G36 rifle at the *Schützenschnur* qualification range at Kandahar Airfield, Afghanistan, 9 March 2014. The *Schützenschnur* is the German armed forces' badge of marksmanship. (Cpl Clay Beyersdorfer/Wikimedia/Public Domain)

CONCLUSION

Developed in the early years of the Cold War, the G3 was a winner in the contest between the assault rifle, as represented by the AK-47 and M16, and the battle rifle, as represented by the FAL, G3 and M14. The anticipation of a penultimate battle between East and West, Communism and Democracy that might occur on the North German Plain made the choice of a rifle capable of longer range and greater striking power seem prudent during the 1950s; however, the success of the AK-47 in insurgencies across the globe and the utility of the M16 during counter-insurgency warfare in Southeast Asia raised questions about the need for the battle rifle. Eventually, the G3 would be replaced by the G36, an assault rifle chambered for the 5.56×45mm cartridge.

Estimates of the number of G3 rifles and copies built range from 7,000,000 to as high as 20,000,000, but a precise figure is difficult to establish with any authority because of licensed and unlicensed production carried out in various countries. Suffice to say: many millions were used by soldiers in around 80 countries. While large numbers of G3s were in service in West Germany and elsewhere during the Cold War and after, the rifle's most sustained combat usage was during the Iran–Iraq War. It was also used in numerous insurgencies and counter-insurgencies, and still turns up in trouble-spots around the world.

Three advantages of the G3's design have lent itself well to use by NATO powers and developing countries around the world. First, the roller-delayed blowback design allows use of a variety of ammunition without adjustment as would be necessary on a gas-operated design. Second, the G3 will keep firing when dirty; especially important for the armies of some developing countries is the fact that cleaning the G3's gas piston after use of corrosive ammunition is not necessary, as there is no gas piston in a roller-delayed blowback system. Third, the G3 is also relatively inexpensive to manufacture and does not require a large, technologically trained workforce.

Critics of the G3 offer various negatives. Many find that the roller-locking system makes recoil more noticeable than with gas-operated weapons. This factor, combined with the G3's weight and poor balance, has made it a difficult rifle for smaller-statured troops to use. Adding to the disadvantages for smaller soldiers, the cocking handle requires substantial strength to pull back. Even for larger soldiers, the G3 is not an especially user-friendly rifle.

Although retained by some armies today, mostly because of the financial burden of replacing it, the G3 has been supplanted in the armed forces of many countries by a 5.56×45mm weapon, such as the M4/M16 or the G36. Even with armies that have chosen a different rifle to succeed the G3 as their primary weapon, some G3s often remain in service to serve as DMRs. The replacement of the G3 in many parts of the world has proven a boon to US civilian shooters, as a large number of the rifles have been turned into parts kits for assembly in the United States on semi-automatic receivers. As a result, these rifles are widely encountered in US gun shops, on ranges and in the hunting fields.

As with the FAL and M14, the G3 might have proven itself if Warsaw Pact forces had rolled through the Fulda Gap during the Cold War. These NATO battle rifles would have outranged the AK-47s in use with the Warsaw Pact forces and given NATO infantryman some advantage. It is doubtful, however, that the range of infantry rifles would have decided such a conflict; it would have depended more on armoured vehicles, tank-killing helicopters and tactical airpower – and lurking in the background would have been tactical nuclear weapons and ultimately strategic nuclear weapons. Fortunately, the G3 and other battle rifles did not have to engage the enemy during World War III.

Nevertheless, with its links to the German assault rifles of World War II and its importance in arming the modern Bundeswehr, as well as many other nations' armies, the G3 ranks as one of the most important military rifles of the 20th century, with some continuing influence into the 21st century. At the time of writing the G3 is still serving in some parts of the world and will likely turn up in insurgencies or in armouries for decades to come.

BIBLIOGRAPHY

Ansari, U. (2016). 'Pakistan Seeks New Service Rifle, Upgraded Ordnance Facilities', available at http://www.defensenews.com/story/defense/land/weapons/2016/03/16/pakistan-seeks-new-service-rifle-upgraded-ordnance-facilities/81882200/

Beeck, C. (2014). 'Germany: From Surplus Exports to Destruction', in Karp, A., ed., *The Politics of Destroying Surplus Small Arms: Inconspicuous Disarmament*. Abingdon: Routledge.

Binda, A. (no date). 'Mozambique 1968–72 Rhodesian and Portuguese Cooperation', available at http://rhodesianforces.org/Mozambique1968-72.htm

Brogan, P. & Zarca, A. (1983). *Deadly Business: Sam Cummings, Interarms and the Arms Trade*. New York, NY: W.W. Norton & Co.

Cann, J.P. (2013). *The Flechas: Insurgent Hunting in Eastern Angola, 1965–1974*. Solihull: Helion.

Cann, J.P. (2016). *The Fuzileiros: Portuguese Marines in Africa, 1961–1974*. Solihull: Helion.

Carlson, T.E. & Golm, D. (1969). 'A Comparative Evaluation of the 7.62mm and 5.56mm, G-3 Assault Rifles'. Memorandum Report No. 1953. Aberdeen Proving Ground, MD.

Deckert, R. (2007). 'Strong and Fast: German Arms in Burma', available at http://www.bits.de/public/articles/kleinwaffen-nl11-07eng.htm

Deckert, R. (2008). 'Heckler & Koch's role in the Thai-Cambodian conflict', available at http://www.rib-ev.de/2008/11/12/daks-small-arms-newsletter-hk-articles-in-english/

Falconer, D. (1998). *First Into Action*. London: Little, Brown & Co.

Gangarosa, G., Jr. (2001). *Heckler & Koch: Armorers of the Free World*. Accokeek, MD: Stoeger.

Johnston, G.P. & Nelson, T.B. (2010). *The World's Assault Rifles*. Lorton, VA: Ironside.

Jones, Richard D., ed. (2007). *Jane's Infantry Weapons, 2007–2008*. Coulsdon: Jane's.

Kenneth, V. (2009). 'Burmese Small Arms Development', in *Small Arms Review*. Available online at http://www.smallarmsreview.com/display.article.cfm?idarticles=1154

McCollum, Ian (2016). 'Riot-Control Trigger Guards on Turkish G3 Rifles', *Forgotten Weapons.com*. https://www.forgottenweapons.com/riot-control-trigger-guards-on-turkish-g3-rifles/

Moore, L.F. (1954). Thirty-eighth Report on Project TS2-2105. Aberdeen Proving Ground.

Popenker, Maxim & Williams, Anthony G. (2004). *Assault Rifles: The Development of the Modern Military Rifle and its Ammunition*. Ramsbury: Crowood.

Rennie, James (1996). *The Operators: On the Streets with 14 Company*. London: Century.

Rimmele, T. (2014). 'German Soldiers Don't Trust Their Battle Rifle', in *War is Boring*, available at https://warisboring.com/german-soldiers-dont-trust-their-battle-rifle-e1070a9a67dc#.e5rcnv7u0

Schroeder, M. & King, B. (2012). 'Surviving the Battlefield: Illicit Arms in Afghanistan, Iraq, and Somalia', in *Small Arms Survey* 2012. Cambridge: Cambridge University Press.

Stevens, R.B. (2006). *Full Circle: A Treatise on Roller Locking*. Cobourg: Collector Grade.

Tomkins, D. (2008). *Dirty Combat: Secret Wars and Serious Misadventures*. London: Mainstream.

Zhou, Yi Le (David) (2016). 'NATO Infantry Weapon Standardization: Ideal or Possibility?' Thesis, Graduate Program in Military and Strategic Studies. Calgary, Alberta, March 2016.

INDEX